This book is a gift from
The Friends of the
Carmel Valley Library

Leopold's Shack and Ricketts's Lab

The publisher gratefully acknowledges the generous contribution to this book provided by Indiana State University.

Leopold's Shack and Ricketts's Lab

The Emergence of Environmentalism

Michael J. Lannoo

UNIVERSITY OF CALIFORNIA PRESS

Berkeley   Los Angeles   London

University of California Press, one of the most distinguished
university presses in the United States, enriches lives around the
world by advancing scholarship in the humanities, social sciences,
and natural sciences. Its activities are supported by the UC Press
Foundation and by philanthropic contributions from individuals
and institutions. For more information, visit www.ucpress.edu.

University of California Press
Berkeley and Los Angeles, California

University of California Press, Ltd.
London, England

Library of Congress Cataloging-in-Publication Data
Lannoo, Michael J.
    Leopold's Shack and Ricketts's Lab : the emergence of environ-
mentalism / Michael J. Lannoo.
        p.   cm.
    Includes bibliographical references and index.
    ISBN 978-0-520-26478-6 (cloth : alk. paper)
    1. Environmentalism—United States—History.   2. Natural
History—United States—History.   3. Ecology—United States—
History.   4. Leopold, Aldo, 1886–1948.   5. Ricketts, Edward
Flanders, 1897–1948.   I. Title.
GE195.L37   2010

333.72092'2—dc22   2009044829

Manufactured in the United States of America

19 18 17 16 15 14 13 12 11 10
10 9 8 7 6 5 4 3 2 1

This book is printed on Cascades Enviro 100, a 100% post
consumer waste, recycled, de-inked fiber. FSC recycled certified
and processed chlorine free. It is acid free, Ecologo certified, and
manufactured by BioGas energy.

For Pete and Angus
Strings and Keyboards:
Keep playing your music,
we'll get things turned around

Every now and then [life] becomes literature—not for long, of course, but long enough to be what we best remember, and often enough that what we eventually come to mean by life are those moments when life, instead of going sideways, backwards, forward, or nowhere at all, lines out straight, tense and inevitable, with a complication, climax, and, given some luck, a purgation, as if life had been made and not happened.

Norman Maclean,
"USFS 1919: The Ranger, the Cook, and a Hole in the Sky"

CONTENTS

PREFACE

A broad interdisciplinary approach is to be expected from ecologists, who take the relationships among all things as a first principle. No relationship, no matter how tenuous it appears, is too inappropriate for exploration.[1] Specialization is the fashion of the day, however, and it may be the style of most human thinking for all time. That is, considering human brain architecture, it may be easier for our minds to work within the confines of defined units, or silos in the modern parlance, than it is for us to make broad cross-topic comparisons.

I find it necessary, at times, to lean on heroes, and two of my longtime heroes are the early ecologists Aldo Leopold and Ed Ricketts. When I'm off center, or maybe just want to relax, I turn to these men. Not only have I read everything they have published, but I have also read everything I know to have been published about them. I have visited their shacks and have gotten to know their primary scholars—Leopold and Ricketts are men who have stood, and can stand, a lot of study.[2] And I have noticed that even though they were contemporaries, and even though they contributed mightily toward molding the field of observational natural history into the scientific discipline of ecology, there is no single place in any of the works by or about Leopold or Ricketts where the other is mentioned. While I suspect that both Leopold and Ricketts would have been appalled to learn this, they have become silos—big enough and important enough to be self-contained.

The stories of Leopold and Ricketts are, indeed, interesting and important told separately—they were amazingly gifted human beings. Works on Leopold include Curt Meine's 1988 biography *Aldo Leopold: His Life and Work*, which was nominated for a Pulitzer Prize; Bob McCabe's 1987 *Aldo Leopold: The Professor;* Tom Tanner's 1987 collection of essays, *Aldo Leopold: The Man and His Legacy;* J. Baird Callicott's 1987 collection *Companion to A Sand County Almanac: Interpretive and Critical Essays;* and Susan Flader's 1974 *Thinking like a Mountain: Aldo Leopold and the Evolution of an Ecological Attitude toward Deer, Wolves, and Forests.*[3] New books about Leopold, such as Julianne Lutz Newton's *Aldo Leopold's Odyssey,* appear on a regular basis.[4]

Ed Ricketts has had his own admirers. In 1973, Richard Astro published *John Steinbeck and Edward F. Ricketts: The Shaping of a Novelist,* and in 1976 Astro wrote *Edward F. Ricketts* as part of Boise State University's Western Writers Series.[5] Joel Hedgpeth's two-volume set *The Outer Shores,* published in 1978, pulled together edited versions of Ricketts's unpublished papers and offered an objective, firsthand look at the man (as opposed to the "Doc" of John Steinbeck's legend).[6] Hedgpeth knew Ricketts both personally and professionally, and provides an account that is fresh and honest. Hedgpeth's volumes were covered in an article in the Whole Earth Catalog's literary magazine *CoEvolu-*

tion Quarterly.[7] Recently, Katie Rodger, working closely with Ed Ricketts Jr. and the Ricketts family, published two extraordinary volumes of original Ricketts material: her 2002 *Renaissance Man of Cannery Row: The Life and Letters of Edward F. Ricketts* and her 2006 *Breaking Through: Essays, Journals, and Travelogues of Edward F. Ricketts* (with Ricketts listed as posthumous coauthor).[8] In 2004, Eric Enno Tamm published his enthusiastic and insightful *Beyond the Outer Shores: The Untold Odyssey of Ed Ricketts, the Pioneering Ecologist Who Inspired John Steinbeck and Joseph Campbell.*[9]

Considering these men today, I am struck that playing one off the other might give us, now, a better sense of what it was like to be them, then—at a point in time when the new discipline of ecology was emerging from the older field of natural history, and when advances in ecological theory were being driven by natural history observations. Viewing Leopold and Ricketts simultaneously makes it easier to understand these men in terms of their setting—what Michael Lewis has called "the accomplishments of men in combination with their circumstances."[10] By telling their stories together, comparing and contrasting, a different picture emerges from those presented in the works by or about either man, and we gain a different perspective. In fact, as I hope to show, we gain a perspective on the world that is larger than the field of ecology, a perspective that should be of interest to us all.

ACKNOWLEDGMENTS

This work in this form would not have been possible without Mike Mossman, Lisa Hartman, and their son, Angus, who kindly opened up their house, and their Baraboo Hills bluff, to me. Curt Meine, the preeminent Leopold scholar, and Katie Rodger, the preeminent Ricketts scholar, agreed to rendezvous at the Mossmans' for dinner and an evening campfire. The next morning we gathered at the Leopold Legacy Center and discussed, no holds barred, the pros and cons of this project. That afternoon, under a fresh Indian summer sky, we contemplated the sense of the morning as we drank microbrews, ate brats, and listened to folk music (mostly by Curt's group) under oak trees that were old when Leopold was alive.

Through Mike and Curt, I introduced an early draft of this manuscript to two of Aldo Leopold's children, Nina Leopold Bradley and Carl Leopold; in California, Katie passed it along to Ed Ricketts Jr. The fact that the children of Aldo Leopold and Ed Ricketts read and approved of this effort suggests that I've succeeded in approaching some historical truth; they lived in, and know, this world that I can only read about and imagine. I am struck with, and in awe of, the kindness they've shown me, and the grace with which they conduct their lives.

David Null, the director of archives at the University of Wisconsin Library, made Leopold's Shack journals and other artifacts available. Susie and Pete—thanks for joining the quest. Rafe Sagarin kindly provided a preprint of his article on Ricketts and the collapse of the sardine industry.

I cannot express the depth of my appreciation for the considered comments on or about early drafts of this manuscript from Nina Leopold Bradley, Carl Leopold, Ed Ricketts Jr., Curt Meine, Katie Rodger, Joe Eastman, Bill Souder, Mike Mossman, Lisa Hartman, Joe Mitchell, Dave Bradford, Alisa Gallant, Shelly Grow, Tim Knab, Priya Nanjappa, Warren Vander Hill, Ann Bovbjerg, Ken Lang, and Susie Lannoo—these are people who care. So does Eric Engles from EditCraft; how can one person be a master of both the big picture and the small detail? Jeannine Richards, communications coordinator for the Aldo Leopold Foundation, provided the cover photograph of Aldo Leopold, which is used with permission of the Aldo Leopold Foundation. Ed Ricketts Jr., through Katie Rodger, provided the cover photograph of Ed Ricketts, which is used with permission of Ed Ricketts Jr.

Thanks to Sharon Hermann for introducing me to Ed Ricketts through *The Log from the Sea of Cortez* when I was an undergraduate at the Iowa Lakeside Laboratory. During my first visit to Ed Ricketts's Lab I was studying with the late Walter Heiligenberg at the Scripps Institute of Oceanography; Gayle Garman, a graduate-student buddy of mine, joined in the pilgrimage. I can't say when I first learned of Aldo Leopold; his aura was everywhere always in the old Animal Ecology Department at Iowa State University, but I will never forget the day several years later when I first saw the Shack; I was with Mike, Lisa, Angus, and Curt, and later that afternoon we visited Nina.

The Iowa Lakeside Lab, in Okoboji, now a hundred years old, is the place where the ideas of Ricketts and Leopold—an approach to ecology and to life based on natural history—came together for me, although that was some time ago and I didn't know it at the time. As I look around, I find I'm living the old Steinbeck and Ricketts quote: "We sat on a crate of oranges, and thought what good [people] most biologists are. . . . "

Introduction

At about 10:30 A.M. on Wednesday, April 21, 1948, north of Baraboo, Wisconsin, Aldo Leopold left the property he dubbed the Shack to fight a brush fire that threatened his beloved pine plantings, and perhaps the Shack itself. An hour or so later, a mile east of the Shack, while reinforcing a neighbor's wetland as a firebreak, he had a heart attack, lay down, crossed his arms over his chest, and died.[1] According to his daughter Estella, who was nearby, the fire burned lightly over him. Leopold regularly carried in his shirt pocket a little notebook for recording his observations. The tiny red, green, and black plaid notebook he was using when he died had its cover melted and its pages charred, and Curt Meine noticed that for a long time after Leopold's death when you opened the little book it smelled like prairie smoke.[2]

Seventeen days later on Saturday, May 8, in Monterey, California, Ed Ricketts slipped quietly out of his lab, Pacific Biological Laboratories, to buy steaks and salad fixings to feed the friends who had gathered (as they always did) for beers and socializing.

He started his car, drove southeast three blocks past the sardine canneries and under their trademark crossovers, along the street formally named Ocean View Avenue and known around the world as Cannery Row, and then turned right up a steep hill to cross the Southern Pacific Railway track. He didn't see or hear the Del Monte Express, the evening train from San Francisco, coming from his left. The steam engine struck the driver's side of the car and, as his best friend, John Steinbeck, wrote, "The cow-catcher buckled in the side of the automobile and pushed and ground and mangled it a hundred yards up the track before the train stopped."[3] Ricketts was lucid but beginning to feel shock when they pulled him from the wreck. He was taken to the hospital and operated on, patched up and spleen removed. But he never regained full consciousness, and three days after the accident, on Tuesday, May 11, three weeks minus a day after Aldo Leopold died, Ed Ricketts stopped fighting and finally succumbed to his injuries. Added Steinbeck: "as happens so often with men of large vitality, the energy and the color and the pulse and the breathing went away silently and quickly, and he died."

Although nobody knew it then, in the short span of three weeks the world had lost two of its greatest thinkers, knowing, visionary men who observed the way the world was, saw the way it was going, and said something about it. Two men who were grounded in natural history, and who would help to lay a practical and philosophical foundation for the environmental movement that arose decades later. Two men who never met, midwestern boys, born ten years and two hundred miles apart, who died twenty days and twenty-two hundred miles apart. Between Leopold and Ricketts, time shrank and space grew.

In the early twentieth century, ecology was in its infancy, not far from its roots in natural history. The scientific study of life and its relationships arose simultaneously from both a broad basic curiosity about how the world works and a narrow practical need to understand commercial biological stocks. At this time, especially in the recently settled United States,[4] civilization began to comprehend that the world and its creatures, many of whom were of extreme importance to humans, were not infinite, and that some form of understanding and self-control was necessary to ensure their continued existence. Land was set aside, game laws enacted, and a handful of extraordinarily bright, fabulously talented biologists—including but not restricted to Leopold and Ricketts—began to explore the relationships among the various forms of life on Earth using the principles of science. Aldo Leopold and Ed Ricketts worked at a time when *ecology* was a word so new to the world of ideas that they themselves rarely used it.

The overarching interest they shared was in the ecological relationships of humans with the world at large. The word *öcologie* is a mid-nineteenth-century term coined by a German, Ernst Haeckel; but the concept that species are interdependent has been slow to sink in. The extension of this concept—the one that so interested Leopold and Ricketts—that human beings are also dependent on other species has been even slower to sink in (and to observe the behavior of people in today's society, mostly it hasn't). Unlike most historical figures, whose ideas reflect the thinking of their era, many thoughts of Leopold and Ricketts have become more relevant with the passage of time.

Leopold and Ricketts came from great schools: Leopold from the Yale School of Forestry, Ricketts from the University of Chicago. They had celebrated mentors: Leopold was guided by Gifford Pinchot; Ricketts was inspired by Warder Clyde Allee. Astonishingly, neither Leopold nor Ricketts held a PhD degree, the usual prerequisite for their chosen fields. Despite this, Ricketts's ideas were mined by graduate students at Stanford's Hopkins Marine Station, and Leopold supervised the training of nine doctoral students.[5] Both men were born in the Midwest, but Ricketts settled on the West Coast (giving the present effort a "surf-and-turf" flavor). They both kept extensive journals.

Leopold and Ricketts did much of their best thinking in shacks, and this was no accident. Leopold's Shack is more famous, but Ricketts, too, worked out of a shack, the only kind of building he could afford after his laboratory burned down. Among early environmentalists, Leopold and Ricketts were not alone in their preference for simple dwellings. Thoreau lived in a cabin; so did Muir. In fact, Muir diverted Yosemite Creek under his so he could listen to the sound of water below the floor (and as a bonus hear calling frogs).[6] Shacks, cabins, and their ilk, including shanties, huts, cottages, trailers, and even some laboratory buildings, reflect the architecture of a country founded in frontier. Shacks are outposts in wilderness. Shacks are also places for freethinkers, people who want to get away from it all.

For Leopold and Ricketts, access to shacks gave them a huge advantage. These simple buildings allowed basic needs to be met while positioning them near the environments and people they loved, and these dwellings allowed them to observe, study, and engage with the natural world on an almost daily basis. And because Leopold and Ricketts could focus on their interests without the energy and time constraints of working from a distance, there was more time for contemplation. Thoughts from shacks naturally tend to emanate outward; the structures themselves are so simple and utilitarian that there is no preoccupation with them, or the small snippets of life carried on within them. As Eric Engles has pointed out, shacks—being financially, structurally, aesthetically, and energetically simple—allow an uncluttered perspective on life's larger questions.[7] The shacks of Leopold and Ricketts gave these naturalists-cum-ecologists the freedom to gain perspective on a much more needy and greedy society.

The concept of "shack" also works as metaphor for a grounded, bottom-up, facts-based approach to thinking and to living. As Apsley Cherry-Garrard once pointed out, living and working out of a remote hut, he and his companions had "just enough to eat and keep us warm, no more—no frills nor trimmings: there is many a worse and more elaborate life. The necessities of civilization were luxuries to us . . . the luxuries of civilization satisfy only those wants which they themselves create."[8] As such, the lessons learned from these buildings extend beyond the realm of science. It is not surprising to learn that Aldo Leopold's Shack and Ed Ricketts's Laboratory have become gathering points for all kinds of people with biological and philosophical interests. Each building not only has a classic scientific literature generated from the inside looking out—these buildings were, after all, base camps for exploration—but each also has a deep philosophical literature from the outside looking in. As a consequence, these structures have become shrines. And as with shrines everywhere, pilgrims come to visit, hoping to experience some of the enchantment of the place and perhaps capture the magic of its inhabitants.

There is no splendor in these buildings. Each is small, simple, by and large uninsulated, built of soft wood—mostly pine. They have always leaked (rain through the roof in the case of the Lab, and both rain and snow in the case of the Shack).[9] Despite being huddled in a pine-oak woodlands, Leopold's Shack was once hit by lightning. The Shack was the family weekend and free-time getaway, close enough to the Leopolds' home in Madison that they could come and go as desired, except when gasoline was rationed during World War II. Ricketts's Lab was also his home, occupied always while he was in town, and sometimes when he wasn't. Today, each building is used but not inhabited. The Shack is located in the Upper Midwest, on the southern bank of the Wisconsin River; the Lab backs up on the Pacific Ocean, on the northern shore of the Monterey Peninsula. Each sits near a shoreline; they are "edgy." Thousands have visited each building; few have visited both. They are simple structures representing truly great people with timeless ideas. And although there is little grandeur in their appearance, there is much grandeur in their presence.

As we are about to see, Leopold and Ricketts were vastly different men, with different lifestyles, different views of the world, and different ways of doing science.[10] It is curious, therefore, that these two early ecologists could be living such different lives in parallel—thinking mostly similar but sometimes complementary thoughts "lined out straight, tense and inevitable" from different perspectives.[11] They were forming big concepts about the relationships of humans with the larger world, ideas that would (in my best Norman Maclean run-on style) form the buds that created the flowers that spread the seeds of the ideas upon which the future of humanity now depends.

Leopold and Ricketts had different approaches, but working out of shacks they came to the same conclusion: that the salvation of society, and perhaps of the human species, can be found in the workings of natural history. This is a lesson not just for their time, but for all time. Despite its absence from much of modern culture, the notion that humans cannot forever place themselves above Earth's ecosystems represents what Ricketts once called the most powerful idea of the twentieth century and "perhaps the key to the future."[12]

CHAPTER ONE

Out of the Midwest

Leopold and Ricketts shared a midwestern upbringing. Rand Aldo Leopold was born on January 11, 1887, in Burlington, Iowa, to first cousins Carl and Clara Leopold. Aldo was the eldest of four Leopold children; Marie was born in 1888, Carl Jr. in 1892, and Frederic in 1895. His father began his career as a traveling salesman, selling barbed wire to western ranchers, before settling down to run the Rand and Leopold Desk Company. And although "Carl had hardly ever used a desk, much less built one," he was "a businessman of the highest integrity. His approach was as simple as it was risky: he wanted to build the best desk that he could, and if he could make a profit at it, so much the better."[1] The company made roll-top desks constructed of cherry, oak, and walnut, known for their enduring quality. The company's motto, emblazoned on its stationery, was "Built on Honor to Endure."

Edward Flanders Robb Ricketts was born on May 14, 1897, in Chicago, Illinois, to Abbott and Alice Ricketts. Ed was the eldest of the three Ricketts children; his sister, Frances, was born in 1899, his brother, Thayer, in 1902. His father made a modest income as an accountant and a salesman. In her journal Frances noted, "most of their paternal relatives were ministers, while many in their mother's family were storekeepers. Not a really poor person on either side . . . I wonder what is the matter with our branch of the family in this generation?"[2]

Both Leopold and Ricketts showed early the promise of the men they would become. Young Aldo was "a precocious student, interested in many things, and good at most everything he was interested in."[3] Leopold's interest in the natural world reflected his family's activities, and growing up along the Mississippi River and its waterfowl flyway gave him every opportunity to explore and, later, hunt. Curt Meine writes, "The early observer atop Burlington's bluffs gained an eyelevel view of one of the most spectacular wildlife displays the continent has ever offered. The hunter in the marshes below gained one of its most promising shots."[4]

In order to provide relief for the hay fever that Aldo's mother suffered, every August the Leopold family traveled to the north end of Lake Huron, spending six weeks or so on Les Cheneaux Islands. It was "land rich in the raw material of adventure, and wild enough to inspire the imagination."[5] Aldo's youngest brother, Frederic, recalled, "In our young minds, we imagined that we were at the jumping off place where to the north an endless wilderness extended to Hudson Bay and the arctic."[6]

In high school, Aldo was introduced to the "disciplined natural science that he would eventually make his life's work."[7] In the process he honed his considerable artistic ability by making detailed maps and anatomical drawings. From his English teacher, Miss Rogers, he learned a deep appreciation for the written word. Leopold also developed an interest in forestry, and at the time the only school of forestry in the country was at Yale University. In 1904 he shipped off to Lawrenceville Preparatory School in Lawrenceville, New Jersey, where he spent an academic year and a half laying the foundation for an Ivy League education, although he noted, "The instruction in English and History is much inferior to that of the [Burlington] High School."[8]

Ed Ricketts was "from birth, a child of intelligence and rare charm. . . . He began speaking very young and began using whole but simple sentences before he was a year old."[9] His family lived in a rough section of Chicago, and their worried mother sheltered them. His sister wrote, "We spent hours at home in pre-school days with our noses pressed against the window pane looking out."[10] Under these conditions all the Ricketts children became enthusiastic readers. As Ed recalled much later, in a letter to Harcourt, Brace, "At the age of six, I was ruined for any ordinary activities when an uncle who should have known better gave me some natural history curios and an old zoology textbook. Here I saw for the first time those magical and incorrect words 'coral insects.'"[11]

Ricketts's parents were devout Episcopalians, and Ed was a choirboy.[12] When he was ten, his father accepted a job in Mitchell, South Dakota, and moved the family there. They stayed only a year before moving back to Chicago, but for young Ed it was a crucial year. He spent his time outdoors and "collected and studied birds, insects and every other form of life he encountered."[13]

In school, Ricketts was known as "the walking dictionary." Though not athletic, he was strong and compact, "hardening himself" by taking cold morning "plunges" and exercising in the evenings. His sister Frances wrote, "By the time he was 11 or 12 he also slept outdoors on the ground in our back yard much of the time rolled in blankets, without 'even a tent,' until winter. . . . It was part of his program to sleep out, even during storms. Our parents were pleased when they were able to bribe him to sleep indoors during the coldest weather."[14] In high school, Ed enjoyed and excelled in both science and humanities courses, and began making the cross-disciplinary connections that would character-ize his thinking for the rest of his life.[15]

Despite these similarities, there were deep personality differ-ences between the two youths. Leopold was shy, especially when it came to interacting with girls; among his closest companions were the family dogs. In high school "Aldo remained solitary in his ways, not antisocial, not social." His brother, Frederic, noted, "He did not think he was cut from common cloth, and he wasn't."[16] In contrast, Ricketts was outgoing and charming; people were drawn to him. "Revered among his friends as a talker—some called him the Buddha or the Mandarin, both because of his habit of sitting cross-legged on his bed, quietly nodding and smiling in response to whatever nonsense was going on in the room at the time, and when he spoke his words were wise."[17] Women were attracted to him, and he was attracted to women. Ricketts always thought of himself as a common man, and several of his later associates were bums and prostitutes (Ricketts's motives with these women were not related to their profession, and he did not "befriend" them through the usual method of transaction fees).

Leopold and Ricketts attended first-rate universities, but as with their personalities, college life could not have been more different for the two young men. In September 1905, Leopold began his studies at Yale.[18] In 1900 an endowment from the fam-ily of the nation's leading forester, Gifford Pinchot, had allowed Yale to establish the first graduate school of forestry in the United

States. "The school promoted Pinchot's doctrine of scientific resource management and what Samuel Hayes has characterized
as the Progressive Era's 'gospel of efficiency.'"[19] Leopold excelled
at Yale—the rigor, formality, and status of the program suited
him—although in February 1908 he was put on probation for
skipping classes.[20] He put the reprimand behind him and graduated that spring with a bachelor's degree. Leopold returned to
Yale that fall, and in 1909 graduated with his master's degree
in forestry. That March, Leopold and all thirty-four classmates
boarded the SS *Comus* in New York and steamed to New Orleans
on their way to Texas for a final assignment and their civil service
exams.[21]

Ricketts enrolled at Illinois State Normal University, outside
Bloomington, in 1915.[22] He took courses that academic year but
left school to gain some space following an affair with an older,
married woman.[23] He traveled, finding work as a bookkeeper at a
country club in El Paso, Texas, and as a surveyor's assistant in New
Mexico. In September 1917, despite having flat feet, Ricketts was
drafted into the army and served back in Illinois at Camp Grant,
as a clerk in the Medical Corps. He was discharged after the
Armistice in March 1919. That summer, Ricketts enrolled at the
University of Chicago, where he concentrated on biology courses.

Ricketts was never concerned with the formal requirements
for graduation; he simply wanted to be exposed to knowledge
and to new forms of thinking. At the University of Chicago he
became a part-time student while working at the Sinclair Refin-
ing Company. He left school to escape another romantic predica-
ment during the summer and fall quarters of 1920 and "put on
a little knapsack and . . . walked through Indiana and Kentucky
and North Carolina and Georgia clear into Florida."[24] As Joel

Hedgpeth observes in a footnote, "It was characteristic of Ed that when he read about John Muir's selection of the cemetery as the safe place to spend the night in superstitious regions he immediately followed suit."[25]

Ricketts returned to the University of Chicago in 1921, where he was to be forever inspired by Warder Clyde Allee, best known for his 1931 book *Animal Aggregations*.[26] Allee was Ricketts's favorite teacher, and for the professional Ricketts, everything began with Allee. The student made an equally strong impression on the professor. Even twenty-nine years later, in an interview with Hedgpeth, Allee remembered Ricketts as "a member of a small group of 'Ishmaelites' who tended sometimes to be disturbing, but were always stimulating."[27]

After the fall quarter of 1922, Ricketts left the University of Chicago without formally withdrawing. He had gotten married on August 19 to Anna Barbara Maker, who had moved to Chicago from Pennsylvania, and "impending fatherhood obliged him to consider more reliable ways of making a living."[28]

After college, Leopold and Ricketts continued their separate career paths. When Leopold graduated from Yale, he went to work for Pinchot in the U.S. Forest Service. Leopold was "one of an elite corps of scientifically trained professionals who would develop administrative policies and techniques for the fledgling agency charged since 1905 with responsibility for managing the national forests."[29] Leopold was assigned to the new Southwestern District, embracing Arizona and New Mexico territories. In 1923 Ricketts and his former college roommate, Albert E. Galigher, arranged to move to Monterey and, with Galigher's money, set up a biological supply business. Ricketts postponed departing Chicago until his son, Ed Jr., was born.

CHAPTER TWO

From Forester to Professor

Aldo Leopold's midwestern upbringing and Ivy League education had prepared him to be a professional, but even from the
beginning of his career he showed signs of being much more than
that. Curt Meine writes that as a young professional, Leopold was
"competent, devoted, and eager." And while it is true that as a
graduate of the Yale School of Forestry he was a disciple of Gifford Pinchot, Leopold was different. His attitudes "were too inde-
pendent to be dominated by anyone, or by any idea. He did not
often express those attitudes; they were not yet fully developed,
the prevailing philosophies sufficed." But Leopold kept his mind
open, "ensuring that when new light would be needed, he could
help to shed it."[1]

On July 19, 1909, Leopold reported to the year-old Apache
National Forest just outside Springerville, in the Arizona Territory. His title was forest assistant, and he carried out reconnais-
sance and timber cruising. He had problems with his crew. As
Meine states, "The problem was not simply that he was a green-

horn, but that he was confidently inflicting his greenness on the others."[2] It was about this time that Leopold's crew shot a female wolf and he saw in her dying eyes a "fierce green fire" that would haunt him the rest of his life.[3]

Leopold had two other dramatic, life-changing experiences during the two decades he spent with the U.S. Forest Service in the Southwest. The first occurred during the spring of 1911. While on temporary duty in Albuquerque, Leopold met Estella Bergere. Soon afterward, he took an assignment as deputy supervisor at the Carson National Forest, near Anonito, Colorado; he quickly became supervisor. Aldo courted Estella long distance, and on October 9, 1912, they were married in Santa Fe. Meine writes, "she sensitized him to an extreme degree. She inspired him in his thought, in his senses, in his work, and in his ambitions, and she would continue to do so for thirty-six years."[4]

Leopold's second experience was much less pleasant. In early April 1913, after settling a range dispute in the Jicarilla district, Leopold got caught in a spring storm that lasted two days and included hail and bouts of rain, sleet, and snow.[5] As he rode back his knees became so swollen that he had to slit his leather riding boots. When Leopold finally returned to headquarters on April 23, his face and limbs were swollen, and two days later he took the train to see physicians in Santa Fe. During the train ride he became "horribly swollen" and arrived in Santa Fe barely alive; had he stayed at Carson much longer he likely would have died. He was suffering from a case of acute nephritis (Bright's disease). His kidneys had failed, and his symptoms were due to renal salt and water retention.

His recovery took more than sixteen months. Six weeks after his diagnosis he had regained enough strength to board a train with Estella and travel to Burlington, Iowa, where he convalesced at his parents' home and she gave birth to their first son, Starker. At his parents' house, Leopold sat on the east porch resting, reading, and contemplating the view of the Mississippi River far below. He had always been a solitary thinker; here his thoughts turned to conservation and back to Carson National Forest, and it wasn't long before these thoughts began to include concern for wild game. In February 1914, Leopold was allowed to return to the Southwest, but not to Carson. He finally resumed work six months later.

We can ask, What do people like Leopold—with big brains they know how to use—do when they have faced death and are on the road to recovery, but are forced to be physically inactive for a long period of time? You can bet they think, and you can bet they ask themselves about the important things in life. Having faced their own mortality, they consider how, with the time they have left, whether short or long, they can make a difference. When Leopold returned to the Southwest, he brought with him a new sense of purpose.

Resuming work, Leopold shifted emphasis from forestry to wildlife assignments and began developing a new program based on cooperative game management that became a model for Forest Service activities nationwide. At this time, Leopold's approach to game management was based on principles of forest management, which was essentially a quantitative assessment of a natural resource. "Game could bring nearly as much income to the region as timber or grazing uses of the forests, he calculated, if enough effort, intelligence, and money were committed to develop the resource . . . the idea was not merely to rear game and then release it to be shot, but to manipulate habitat so that, in effect, the game raised itself."[6] A key feature of Leopold's new program was the extermination of top predators, including wolves and mountain lions.

For his successes in the Southwest, Leopold received a letter of congratulation from Theodore Roosevelt in January 1917. In July, Hornaday's Permanent Wild Life Protection Fund awarded Leopold its gold medal. In his acceptance speech, Leopold stated that the ideal was "to restore to every citizen his inalienable right to know and love the wild things of his native land. We conceive of these wild things as an integral part of our national environment, and are striving to promote, restore, and develop them not as so many pounds of meat, nor as so many things to shoot at, but as a tremendous social asset, as a source of democratic and healthful recreation to the millions of today and the tens of millions of tomorrow."[7]

The United States entered World War I in April 1917, and because of his age, questionable health, and family (Luna, and later Nina and Carl, were born in New Mexico), Leopold was excused from the draft. About this time, Leopold found a quotation in *Harper's* magazine that became his credo: "We . . . want culture, by which I mean no mere affectation of knowledge, nor any power of glib speech, or idle command of the fopperies of art and literature, but, rather, an intelligent interest in the possibilities of living."[8]

In January 1918, Leopold left the Forest Service to take the position of secretary of the Albuquerque Chamber of Commence. He meant this move to be temporary, until the end of the war, when the Forest Service could again pursue its prewar priorities, and indeed it was. In August 1919, Leopold rejoined the Forest Service as an assistant district forester, responsible for managing

20 million acres. Some within the forest service felt that he had been promoted beyond his experience.[9]

In the next few years Leopold worked on a wilderness protection program and soil erosion problems. It was the idea of wilderness preservation that initiated Leopold's departure from Pinchot's utilitarian philosophy.[10] Leopold felt that the condition of the forest should be the measure of effective Forest Service management. Consistent with this notion, Leopold formulated a regional working plan that designated the Gila Wilderness Area, the first wilderness area in the nation. Meine writes, "here was a sign of cultural foresight, a willingness to let a wild place be. While serving the self-interest of those, including and especially Leopold, who enjoyed the experience of untamed country, it was, in the larger view of history, a quiet act of national magnanimity. No European nation ever could, or ever would, proclaim such a wilderness."[11]

In the spring of 1924, the director of the Forest Products Laboratory in Madison, Wisconsin, was expected to resign, and in anticipation of an eventual promotion Leopold was offered the position of assistant director. In April, he accepted "for reasons he never fully explained."[12] And by the end of July, Aldo, Estella, and the children—Starker, age ten; Luna, age eight; Nina, age six; and Carl, age four—moved into a house they bought on Van Hise Avenue. Three years later, Estella Jr. was born.

Leopold took responsibility for several important Forest Products Laboratory programs, including promoting closer cooperation among the national forests, reducing forest products industry waste, and encouraging the use of lower-grade tree species in order for forests to be more fully harvested.[13] But this was not his kind of work. As the tedium of his position increased, Leopold looked elsewhere for release. He worked behind the scenes with the Izaak Walton League, one of the most effective conservation groups operating anywhere, for early protection of the Boundary Waters area of northeastern Minnesota.[14] About this time the Leopolds took up archery, an interest that would eventually lead to the purchase of the property he called the Shack, after the lone, decrepit structure standing on it.

In early 1928, four years after Leopold arrived in Madison, the director of the Forest Products Laboratory still had not retired, and it became clear to Leopold that "the longer he remained at the Forest Products Lab, the slimmer his chances for advancement seemed."[15] He took a month's leave in an attempt to finish a manuscript, *Southwestern Game Fields,* and to assess his future. In April he announced he had "no intention to continue in my present place." And as word got out, suitors began appearing. Representatives of the Sporting Arms and Ammunitions Manufacturers' Institute approached Leopold with an offer to conduct a nationwide survey of game conditions. Leopold agreed, and found himself "entering a field which did not even exist."[16] Central to the issue of game was a divide between the old-school approach, represented by the passage of game laws, and the approach Leopold advocated, which was management through the control of environment, with hunting being but one aspect of control.[17] Within months of being on the job, Leopold "began to find evidence of the most important trend of the times: the intensification of agriculture was eliminating food and cover plants required by upland game species."[18]

In September 1928 Leopold returned to Madison, and the University of Wisconsin offered him office space. Leopold hired a secretary, Vivian Horn, who noted, "I was astounded at the amount of data he could collect, and how steadily he could work assembling the data and turning out his reports after his return."[19] In February and March 1929, Leopold delivered a series of lectures on game management through the University of Wisconsin, his first official connection with the institution that would ultimately play such an important role in his life.[20] And acting on an inclination that would culminate with the purchase of the Shack, in late 1929 Leopold acquired a small cabin in Missouri that he would use for quail-hunting vacations.[21]

The result of his association with the Sporting Arms and Ammunitions Manufacturers' Institute, Leopold's *Report on a Game Survey of the North Central States,* was published and distributed in the spring of 1931.[22] It brought him a new measure of respect within the conservation community. While previously acknowledged for his leadership in forestry, wilderness preservation, and wildlife protection, Leopold was now recognized as the most informed game expert in the nation. His command of facts was formidable, his network of friends and colleagues continental. His office became something of a national clearinghouse of information on research, personnel, and publications, an advisory service for federal administrators and dirt farmers alike.[23]

As Meine writes, for the rest of his life Leopold would wear this mantle of leadership.[24] A change had come over his personality since he began the game survey. Wildlife had always been his deepest interest, the motive force of his conservation impulse. When he made it his full-time profession, it took the edge off his youthful egoism. Leopold once wrote to his friend, Paul Pettit, "the fundamental weakness of the game movement so far has been that its leaders gradually come to value their personal prestige more than the game. It has happened to every one of them so far, although they are of course unaware of it."[25] Leopold was determined not to make the same mistake. He was also far ahead of his contemporaries in his comprehensive understanding of the environment and in his approach to environmental problems.

With his report finished, Leopold turned to his next project, the completion of a textbook on game management. He had been planning such a professional book ever since he had abandoned the *Southwestern Game Fields* manuscript. The 1929 series of lectures at the University of Wisconsin provided the rough outline for such a text.

CHAPTER THREE

From Businessman to Sage

Ed Ricketts sought to parlay his midwestern work ethic and his University of Chicago experiences into a career built on nature. After he left Chicago in 1923, Ricketts and his new family settled on the Monterey Peninsula. The year before, Libbie Hyman, a member of the faculty at the University of Chicago, had studied at the Hopkins Marine Station there, and Joel Hedgpeth speculates that it may have been her accounts of the rich seashore life that prompted Galigher and Ricketts to choose the region for their biological supply business; the abundant supply of starfish, worms, and jellyfish could support a "modestly thriving" trade. The proximity of the Hopkins Marine Station—the presence of professionals and a first-rate library—was an added advantage, although as Hedgpeth points out, "it must be said that the prospect of an active commercial collecting business was not too happily contemplated by the people at the marine station."[1]

Ed Ricketts was one of the first biologists to bring the young science of ecology to the Pacific Coast.[2] His ecological viewpoint derived from his mentor, W. C. Allee, who had just published his "Studies in Marine Ecology," summarizing observations and fieldwork at Woods Hole, on Cape Cod.[3] Ricketts carefully studied this work (Hedgpeth suggests that some of the material in it formed the basis of Allee's lectures) and used it to guide his own observations on the Pacific Coast; Ricketts considered Allee's ideas "applicable everywhere." Nevertheless, as Hedgpeth notes, "It was not until [the 1960s, after] the sardines disappeared and state and federal funds began to pour out for research that there was much real effort exerted towards understanding the processes of the sea and the shore."[4]

When Ricketts came to the Pacific Coast, there was no guide to the rich fauna and flora of the shores on which he had to depend for specimens for his supply business. It was difficult to identify the animals and so, almost immediately, he set about trying to rectify this problem—a process that would take fifteen years to complete. He began to collect unknowns and sent specimens to the Smithsonian Institution and to specialists at other museums and universities for identification.

As with any business where customers are distributed, Pacific Biological Laboratories needed a catalog, and Ricketts assembled one. As John Steinbeck wrote, "Once, in getting a catalogue ready, [Ricketts] wanted to advise the trade that he had plenty of hagfish available. Now the hagfish is the most disgusting animal both in appearance and texture, and some of its habits are nauseating. It is a perfect animal horror. But Ed did not feel this because the hagfish has certain functions which he found fascinating. In his catalogue he wrote, 'Available in some quantities, delightful and beautiful hagfish.'"[5]

The 1929–30 catalog (affiliated with the University Apparatus Company of Berkeley; Ricketts's uncle, A. P. Flanders, was its president) listed only sponges, coelenterates, and ctenophores, and included descriptive paragraphs about the zoology of each, with scientific references. This was apparently to be the first of many installments, to proceed in textbook order, but later sections were never published. Customers were promised that line drawings would be replaced by "halftones from photos."[6] But a layman's field guide was needed. Because Ricketts knew the identities of the many specimens he had sent to specialists, his friends urged him to pull one together.

Soon after arriving in Monterey, Ricketts apparently felt he had to counter the objections of people at Hopkins about collecting material by stating in his catalog (dated September 1, 1925), "It should be borne in mind (and it applies especially to local marine forms) that we must, above all else, avoid depleting the region by over-collecting." He continued, "Monterey Bay is probably richer in individuals and species than any other region of like size in the United States, and it would be unfortunate if such a situation were to arise here."[7]

Ricketts carefully observed the creatures in the tide pools, and he never tired of looking at them. He began studying the relation of tides to life on the seashore, and analyzing tidal levels. His love for philosophizing crept into the project when he thought of the primal rhythms of tides that govern all life on Earth. The people at Hopkins began to take notice, and in a few years Ricketts's manuscripts were being consulted and mined by graduate students. Having no need to establish an academic reputation or obtain a degree, Ricketts freely shared his ideas.

During their first years on the coast, Ed and his family lived in Carmel. After a few years, they moved to Pacific Grove, to a cottage on Fourth Street near Junipero. In 1930, John Steinbeck and his wife, Carol, moved into the Steinbeck family cottage on Eleventh Street in Pacific Grove.[8] Steinbeck had heard about Ricketts, and apparently through Jack Calvin, a mutual friend who was a writer and adventurer and who would later become junior author on Ricketts's first book, arranged to meet Ed at Calvin's home.[9] Shortly after, Ricketts hired Carol Steinbeck as a clerical assistant.

John Steinbeck's fascination with biology began many years before his friendship with Ricketts. The two men enjoyed a deep respect for each other, and the influence of Ricketts on Steinbeck is well understood.[10] Ricketts shared with Steinbeck his ideas on biology, ecology, and philosophy, as well as any other topics that arose.[11] Within a few years of meeting Ricketts, Steinbeck became fascinated with the differences in behavior between individual men and men in groups. In a letter to George Albee in 1933, Steinbeck wrote, "if you try to judge a mob nature by the nature of its own men units, you will fail as surely as if you tried to understand a man by studying one of his cells."[12] Richard Astro notes, "Much of Steinbeck's thinking about the group man grew from his interest in aggregational patterns of life in the tidepools," which he studied with Ricketts.[13]

A second important idea that Ricketts introduced to Steinbeck was the notion of "nonteleological" or "is" thinking, a nonjudgmental perspective that Ricketts defined as "concerning itself primarily not with what should be, or might be, but rather what actually 'is,' attempting at most to answer the questions what or how, instead of why—a task in itself rigorously difficult."[14]

Ricketts and Steinbeck shared a deep interest in integrating humans and the environment into a unified whole. This interest expanded when, in 1932, Joseph Campbell moved into a small guesthouse, nicknamed Cannery Cottage, next door to the Pacific Grove home of Ricketts, his wife, Nan, and their three small children.[15] Seven years earlier, in 1925, Carol Steinbeck (then Henning) and her sister, Idell, had met young Joe Campbell on a cruise. Campbell had maintained a correspondence with Idell, and visited her on his solo trip (in his Ford Flivver) from New York to the West Coast.[16] Upon his arrival in Monterey, Campbell and Idell found they had nothing in common, but Campbell and Carol Steinbeck developed a deep, mutual attraction. They had an affair "of the heart" and Steinbeck confronted Campbell. During the exchange, Steinbeck asked Campbell how it happened that he had written to Idell all these years. Campbell told him the story. Steinbeck said, "'Too bad it wasn't Carol.' Campbell then responded, 'Yes, that's one part of the irony of this story.' 'No,' Steinbeck quipped, 'I mean you would have had better letters to read.'"[17]

It was a crucial, formative period in everyone's life. While the older Ricketts contributed much to his relationships with Steinbeck and Campbell, he was also greatly influenced by them. And so, while the formative portion of Aldo Leopold's life proceeded in a reasonably straight and logical progression, the formative portion of Ed Ricketts's life did not. The story of his maturation intertwines and tangles with those of John Steinbeck and Joseph Campbell.[18] The interactions with these talented men reinforced Ricketts's emphases on transgressing disciplinary boundaries, making unexpected connections, and understanding the world holistically.

Ricketts's Lab, besides being a rare source of income for everyone during the Depression (they called it the bank), became an improbable intellectual and cultural mecca. Artists, writers, painters, musicians, scientists, and both graduate students and faculty from Hopkins Marine Station down the street would frequently drop by. Parties occasionally went on for days. Ricketts, Steinbeck, and Campbell would spend hours talking about metaphysics, psychology, art, history, poetry, and literature, especially Goethe's *Faust* (Campbell spoke fluent German and Ricketts is said to have expanded his scientific German to read the masterpiece in its original language) and Robinson Jeffers's "Roan Stallion." Campbell was becoming an authority on mythology and Carl Jung, and talked with Steinbeck about his book manuscript, *To a God Unknown,* which had, as a central theme, the power of nature in human mythmaking. "John has a fine, deep, living quality about his work which ought to ring the bell, I think—if his work is ever discovered," Campbell wrote in his diary at the time.[19]

Ricketts and Campbell also discussed Oswald Spengler's *Decline of the West.* As Tamm writes, Ricketts developed a theory that humanity progresses not in some steady, continuous advance, but rather in "a series of steps followed by long plateaus [in evolutionary biology this is called 'punctuated equilibrium'] in every field."[20] Carol Steinbeck remembered, "Ricketts developed a graph to show the raise in steps and plateaus that ran half way around the office. Every tidbit of information went into it in his very fine, infinitesimal handwriting. It got as far as Spengler."[21]

Ricketts elaborated on this stepwise progression twelve years later in an August 1944 letter to Xenia [Kashevaroff] Cage: "I had supposed that the flow of genius was continuous; that the old duffer handed his torch onto the younger. But it seems not to be that way at all. There are spurts, everyone stimulated everyone else, then the thing dies out, there's a period of sterility, and a new thing pops up. Just like groups of cars along a road at night. Found them on time in 6s or 7s, with occasional stragglers or hurriers in between. Or like the bumps in a corduroy road, fairly symmetrical, road doesn't wear down evenly at all."[22]

Xenia Cage, the wife of the avant-garde composer John Cage, was an important link among members of the Lab group. She was the sister of Sasha, Jack Calvin's wife, and Tal, local artist Ritchie Lovejoy's wife; she was also a former lover of Ricketts's, who had joined Ricketts and Campbell in Juneau on a 1932 trip (about which more below). During the trip Xenia had a platonic, though not completely innocent, relationship with Joseph Campbell, whom she called "a very exciting man . . . I had my little windup phonograph with 'Le Sacre du Printemps' of Stravinsky, and I'd play that . . . and Joe would explain to me, 'Now listen when the flute does this,' etc. Meanwhile I was thinking of quite different things than what the flute was doing."[23] She described an encounter that suggested Campbell was having similar thoughts. Xenia had ducked into a secluded place near the ocean and "took off my upper, to get some sun on a big rock." She then heard splashing and thought it was a seal. To her surprise, out of the sea "came this heavenly, naked Joseph Campbell, glistening with cold icy water. He said, 'Hello, Xenia,' and he came up and sat on a rock with me and we discussed a few things. He was not embarrassed, why should I be?"

Ricketts, Steinbeck, and Campbell were each searching for something—a paradigm—through which they could live a rich, consequential existence. Ricketts had begun to formulate some determinative ideas, while Steinbeck was struggling to find himself. As J. J. Benson writes, "Steinbeck's talent was not intellectual so much as it was perceptual and instinctive."[24] Indeed, Steinbeck appears to have had a "realization, born out of genuine modesty, that he had no great ideas to contribute."[25] At the same time,

Campbell was also confused and depressed.[26] And then, as Tamm describes the moment, like a bolt of lightning, Carol Steinbeck stormed into the house in Pacific Grove. She was terribly excited. "I've got the message of 'Roan Stallion,'" she said and began reciting a passage from the poem by Robinson Jeffers: 'Humanity is the start of the race; I say / Humanity is the mould to break away from, the crust to break through, the coal to break into fire, the atom to be split.'" Tamm continues, "The poem captured the zeitgeist for the young men, echoing their thinking about nature, science, humanity and, ultimately, God."[27] Jeffers had pointed the way forward, and the phrase "Humanity is . . . the crust to break through" became emblematic of the philosophical outlook that Ricketts adopted. Further, Tamm notes, "Jeffers' central theme of an emergent arising from life's tragedies would also resonate throughout Steinbeck's greatest works." And for Campbell, "Roan Stallion" was to become a key to the development of his "life-affirmative philosophy," which centered his thoughts on world mythology and comparative religion, a focus that was to carry him for the rest of his life.

Despite this intellectual ferment, in 1932 Ricketts was alone and unhappy, trying to cope with marital woes (for which he was mostly responsible). During the summer he planned to travel with Jack and Sasha Calvin, who owned a thirty-three-foot boat called the *Grampus.* The three of them were to sail from Puget Sound to Juneau, Alaska, ostensibly to collect a little pink jellyfish *(Gonionemus vertens)* and to conduct a survey of the Inside Passage. On June 26, Ed sent a wire to Jack Calvin that said he'd be there the next day and was bringing Joseph Campbell.

For ten weeks, Ricketts, Campbell, and their friends lived the life of what Tamm has called "metaphysical vagabonds" aboard the *Grampus*. Their conversations often centered on Goethe's *Faust*, Jeffers's "Roan Stallion," or the implications of Spengler's *Decline of the West*. Campbell recounted mythic tales. They took long walks and pondered the totems of the Coast Salish, Kwakiutl, Heiltsuk, and Tlingit that they saw along the shore.[28] They spent time reading and listening to music, and had long discussions, both philosophical and otherwise. Ricketts kept working and typing up his collecting reports, while Campbell read Dostoyevsky's *The Idiot*.

As Tamm describes it, Ricketts and Campbell discussed "the difference between the [evolutionary] forces that had originally shaped the human species versus the forces molding modern man." Both men felt that wilderness, through natural selection, had been "the primary force that influenced the development of the human physique and psyche over thousands of years." However, modern man was increasingly urban, removed from more natural historical forces. They reasoned, "In the city, a person became a cog in a mass machine and life became constricted by social mores. An individual was forced to fit into the rigid pattern of industrial society." Campbell sensed that urban values left a person feeling "spiritually unfulfilled." He felt humanity needed "to break through the crust of urban life to reach 'the life breathing beneath,' to tap the earth below the asphalt"; and that to be well rounded, a person needed to "harness values from the city such as science, art, philosophy, politics, music, and literature, while nature provided physical exertion, freedom, individuality, and vitality."[29]

Tamm continues, "The young men were exploring the tension—Ricketts later called it 'hi-tension'—between civilization and nature, the modern and the primitive, which was tearing at the fabric of contemporary society." Ricketts and Campbell agreed that integrating the best aspects of civilization with a natural perspective offered a path not only to happiness but also to personal fulfillment. Ricketts called the results of this approach "breaking through," and for him the term meant transcending the experiences of everyday life to touch something deeper and more meaningful, something spiritual. Campbell referred to his approach as "civilized primitiveness," and summed it up as follows: "to be without principles; to be free-thinking; to be skeptical of all dogmas—to break, whenever possible, the rule of the Golden Mean; to exercise restraint only for the fear of feeling formal."[30]

Ricketts and Campbell grew close; they admired each other immensely, shared common interests, and bonded over their personal travails.[31] For Campbell, the man seven years his senior was not quite a guru, but a special teacher of consciousness as well as of natural science.[32] He later wrote the 1932 trip brought about "one of the primary personal transformations of a life dedicated to self-discovery."[33] Many of the philosophical conclusions reached during this voyage would resonate in the future work of both men. Much later, Campbell would write to Ricketts, "I have still a deep nostalgia for those wonderful days, when everything that has happened since was taking shape. That was, for me at least, the moment of the great death and re-birth that Jung is always talking about, and all of you who were involved in the 'agony' are symbolic dominants of what is left to me of my psyche. Monterey Peninsula is the Earthly Paradise."[34]

CHAPTER FOUR

Game Management

Leopold's *Report on a Game Survey of the North Central States* received nearly universally positive reviews. "No one," says Curt Meine, "had ever packed so many facts about game and habitat into a single book."[1] Leopold next envisioned a larger book as a companion to, and expansion on, *Report on a Game Survey.*[2] He conceived of the book as a much-needed unifying treatise detailing the history, theory, and practice of game management. He worked tirelessly, and for the first six months of 1931 did almost nothing but assemble the new manuscript.

Later in 1931, the Sporting Arms and Ammunitions Manufacturers' Institute "loaned" Leopold to the State of Iowa, as Iowa sought to pull together a comprehensive, twenty-five-year plan to guide its newly formed Fish and Game Commission.[3] Between trips to Iowa, Leopold sought a publisher for *Game Management.* But the Depression affected the industry and companies did not want to risk releasing books on a subject with no publication history. Leopold offered to advance his own money: "I am willing to make a substantial contribution personally to its publication, and while I cannot prove it, I feel there will be a better demand for it than the average publisher is able to appreciate."[4] Finally, in December, Charles Scribner's Sons agreed to publish *Game Management,* provided Leopold make several edits to reduce production costs and contribute a $500.00 subvention. Leopold agreed and "signed the contract on January 11, 1932, his forty-fifth birthday."[5]

During the second half of 1931, Leopold sent the *Game Management* manuscript out for comment to several experts. While waiting for replies he received a letter from Olaus Murie, the immensely talented, maverick field biologist (and later the author of the *Peterson Field Guide to Animal Tracks*).[6] Murie worked for the U.S. Biological Survey, and based on his field data was deeply concerned about the quality of the science underlying the Survey's predator eradication programs. Murie's supervisors were not thrilled with his conclusions, nor were they confident that Leopold would treat the issue in the manner they wished. Two men whom Leopold greatly respected, however, agreed at least in part with Murie. The Survey's W. L. McAtee wrote, "natural enemies should not be sacrificed merely to insure sport."[7] And Paul Errington, the first leader of the first Fish and Wildlife Co-op Unit, at Iowa State University, concluded that "quail were far more sensitive to food and cover conditions than to the depredations of hawks, owls, and foxes."[8] In the end, Leopold's "Predator Control" chapter in *Game Management* reflected this more open-minded approach. He wrote, "many predator-control operations have been based upon assumed or traditional predator-game relationships, or at best on generalizations supported only by a small number of observations which were, in light of present knowledge, often misinterpreted."[9]

In March 1932, Leopold's funding from the Sporting Arms and Ammunitions Manufacturers' Institute ran out. He had some investments, including stock in the Leopold Desk Company, and although the family was inconvenienced, they were not uncomfortable. Leopold continued to work on the manuscript for *Game Management,* and during the summer months he finished his final revisions and literature updates.

Leopold organized *Game Management* into three sections, on management theory, management technique, and game administration. Starting with a survey of the field's history and purpose, he moved on in the first part to address the properties and range of game populations. In "Management Technique," he outlined the tools available to the game manager, from the creation of refuges to the control of habitat, hunting, and predation. Finally, he examined the business side of game management, ending with a bibliography, a glossary, breeding tables, and an index.

With the publication of *Game Management* Leopold invented the field of wildlife biology. It was the culmination of his professional life since his life-threatening bout with Bright's disease, nearly two decades earlier, and his decision while convalescing to embrace the field.

Meine writes that at this time Leopold was also coming to grips with the philosophical context in which game management principles would apply.[10] While *Game Management* took a clearly utilitarian approach—manipulating natural processes to produce more game—Leopold himself was beginning to look beyond his professional training toward a broader understanding of wildlife, and of the fate of wildlife in the face of a society based on unending economic expansion.

In the now-famous last paragraph of *Game Management* Leopold wrote, "In short, twenty centuries of 'progress' have brought the average citizen a vote, a national anthem, a Ford, a bank account, and a high opinion of himself, but not the capacity to live in high density without befouling and denuding his environment, nor a conviction that such capacity, rather than such density, is the true test of whether he is civilized. The practice of game management may be one of the means of developing a culture which will meet this test."[11]

CHAPTER FIVE

Between Pacific Tides

Amid the ferment of philosophical ideas being explored by Ed Ricketts, John Steinbeck, Joseph Campbell, and their friends at the Lab, practical interests were not neglected. Ricketts continued to work on his tide pool book, ultimately titled *Between Pacific Tides*. Jack Calvin assisted in collecting, proofreading, editing, and providing photographs, while local artist Ritchie Lovejoy contributed detailed drawings of the animals (" . . . and weren't they good!").[1] Ed Jr. helped compile data for and create many of the book's graphs and tables. He remembers the painstaking hours he spent making the circular chart that showed the seasonal diatom production in the Aleutian Islands and Southern California and how his father always had to double-check each calculation himself, not wanting to risk a mathematical error. Ricketts's concern with ecological holism, which he considered the interrelation of animals to one another and their environment, which in turn can "lead us to the borderline of the metaphysical," set the book—and himself—apart from the norm.[2]

We do not know as much as we would like about the time Ricketts spent creating his tide pool book, or how he worked with Jack
Calvin to assemble it, because most of his notes and correspondence
from this period were incinerated in the 1936 Cannery Row fire.
Of this time, Katie Rodger writes, "Though he kept to a rigorous
schedule while completing the book, he remained sociable, finding inspiration in discussions about his progress. Working together
diligently, Ricketts and Calvin assembled a draft . . . by 1931."[3]
According to Hedgpeth, Ricketts modeled his book on an 1874
classic study by Verrill and Smith on the invertebrates of Martha's
Vineyard Sound and Allee's papers on the intertidal invertebrates
of Wood's Hole.[4] Ricketts felt that while even the most intelligent
amateur would not know the scientific name or taxonomic clas-
sification of a particular organism, anyone would easily be able to
identify its habitat. And from these habitat characteristics, using
his book, a collector could then match a newfound specimen with
an illustrated species. It was a novel approach that opened the
world of the seashore to anyone interested in exploring it.

Ricketts's habitats were "protected outer coast" and "open coast,"
both subdivided into rocky shores and sandy beaches; "bay and
estuary," divided into rocky shores, sand flats, eelgrass, and mud
flats; and "wharf piling," either exposed or protected. A final section
on marine plankton was followed by an index and bibliography.

Between Pacific Tides clearly reflected both Ricketts's training
and his personality—where he was at that point in his life. He
said he designed this book "so that it can be used by the sea coast
wanderer who finds interest in the little bugs and would like to
know what they are and how they live. Its treatment will revolt
against the theory that only the dull is accurate and only the tiresome, valuable."[5]

Ricketts's ecological perspective was not fashionable science during the 1930s, as evidenced by one of his early notes: "The whole picture should be stressed, and one's feet should be kept firmly on the ground by frequent actual collecting, by observing how the animals live and by constant open-minded checking. Because too often (in zoology as in all other fields) what are thought of as disciplines operate chiefly as biases—prescribed ways of thinking and of doing, into which the professional may retreat when shocked or challenged by some anomaly."[6]

Ricketts submitted the book with the title *A Natural History of Pacific Shore Invertebrates* to Stanford University Press in late 1931.[7] At some point during its consideration, someone—Hedgpeth suggests it may have been someone at Stanford Press—proposed calling the book *Between Pacific Tides,* and the name stuck.

Dr. W. K. Fisher, a well-respected marine biologist at Hopkins, reviewed Ricketts's manuscript for Stanford University Press. He was unsympathetic and his assessment was harsh. In a stern letter to Professor William Hawley Davie, director of Stanford University Press, on December 2, 1931, Fisher wrote, "I read the manuscript with somewhat mixed emotions. The facts are authentic so far as I could see and on the whole it was fairly well written, barring a certain vulgarity in places which doubtless can be eliminated by the Editor." He then aired his major complaint, "The method of taking up the animals from the standpoint of station and exposure on the seashore seems at first sight very logical but from the practical standpoint it seems to me not particularly happy. Both Professor MacGinitie and I were quite frank with Mr. Ricketts on this score." Fisher ended his review, "In any event I think the manuscript should be read by a professional zoologist. It must be remembered that neither of the authors can be classified in this category, although Mr. Ricketts is a collector of considerable experience."[8]

It was a severe rebuke from two major figures of Pacific Coast biology—Fisher was director of Stanford's Hopkins Marine Station; G. E. MacGinitie was director of Caltech's Kerckhoff Marine Laboratory. Although both scientists would occasionally have a drink with Ricketts, they seemed to hold his ecological ideas in low esteem, a view they probably held for the whole field of ecology. But Ricketts had an inner toughness and was not intimidated by this (or any other) criticism; he tested and revised the manuscript, adding sections, such as one on tides as an environmental factor, while keeping faithful to his overall ecological perspective.[9]

When Joseph Campbell joined Ricketts and the Calvins on the *Grampus* expedition to the Outer Shores (Ricketts's term for the Pacific coast of Canada and southeastern Alaska), during the summer of 1932, Ricketts and Calvin were working on revisions to *Between Pacific Tides*. They asked Campbell for his advice, which he gave, but according to Hedgpeth, who does not elaborate, his comments did not always go over well with Calvin.[10]

In redrafting the book, Ricketts wanted, as he described it, to travel the "knife edge"—to write "an account interesting to the layreader, and useful alike to the zoologist." But such a populist approach to science was particularly frowned upon in academia (and still is). Fisher remained unimpressed. "I have found few, very few, who can travel the knife edge," he wrote in his second review, in 1936.[11] Fisher suggested that the work would be more interesting to amateurs than to serious zoologists.

As a concession to Fisher, Ricketts developed a short "zoological introduction" in which he applied Cabrera's Law of ecological incompatibility to the seashore. (Cabrera's Law, which Ricketts

quoted from the March 1935 *Biological Abstracts,* says, "In the same
locality . . . directly related animal forms always occupy different
habitats or ecological stations. . . . Related animal forms are ecologically incompatible, and the incompatibility is the more profound
the more directly they are related.") This was a "startling perception" on the part of Ricketts, according to Hedgpeth, because the
concept had yet to be applied to marine biology. Fisher's harsh reaction to the zoological introduction eventually led to its removal.
The omission of Cabrera's Law, according to Hedgpeth, "may well
have delayed progress in marine ecology of the Pacific Coast for
decades." Despite Fisher's rebuke, Stanford finally approved publication of *Between Pacific Tides.*[12] Still, Ricketts had to overcome
a series of setbacks before the book was actually published. On
December 27, 1938, Ricketts wrote to Swedish biologist Torsten
Gislen, "As unbelievable as it sounds, that shore book will soon be
out. It cannot possibly be held up much longer. I never saw such a
slow outfit as Stanford University Press, and of course lately, since
the [Cannery Row] fire, I've had little opportunity for me to do
the things they wanted me to do with the checking etc." Ricketts
continued, "Now for six months it has been in page proof also, and
there only remained the revision and checking of the alphabetical
index. I hadn't time for the considerable work required, but during
these holidays friends have been helping me, and it will be done
soon."[13]

Slowly, frustration turned to joy. On April 25, 1939, he wrote
to Virginia Scardigli—an artist's model who was a great friend
and part of the Lab group—in typical Ed-speak, "What is tides,
and why are they Between Pacific? . . . Yes, I heard there was a
book out. And little as you'd believe it, I was one of the last to
know. With its customary delicacy, Stanford kept its midwifery

hidden from me, until Dr. Light at UC who is already using it in his classes, wrote me a letter of congratulation. But then, when I wrote to Mr. Stanford himself suggesting the mother-father would like to see the bouncing child, they advised that Light had received unbound copy only, so it's alright." Later in the same letter Ricketts wrote, "Nice if I'd make some money on the things, but no royalties at all for first 500 copies, then 10%. So if, in my lifetime, I get 10¢ an hour for the time put into that job, I'll be lucky. But even that's better than nothing."[14]

Tamm writes that in *Between Pacific Tides,* Ricketts manages to draw in his readers by explaining how grand lessons can be learned from these seemingly insignificant tide pool worlds; how, for example, the observation of species aggregations "may conceivably make understandable the evolutionary background behind the gregariousness of animals, even human beings." Tamm echoes the feelings of almost everyone who has read *Between Pacific Tides* when he writes, "The book, like the tide pools it explores, teems with life, with rich, detailed imagery, humor and whimsy, experimentation, mysticism, scientific discovery, cosmic questions. The qualities that make the work truly unique, 'the first work of its kind' as one scientist described it, came from the boundless curiosity and, perhaps, the touch of genius within Ed Ricketts."[15]

Between Pacific Tides is considered a classic in the literature of marine biology, and with more than a hundred thousand copies sold is one of the best-selling books ever published by Stanford University Press. It received excellent peer reviews in several high-profile journals and is still in print, now in its fifth edition. *Between Pacific Tides* has become immensely popular over the years and has become a model for many subsequent seashore books. These are remarkable accomplishments for a scientific work initially rejected and finally published a long three years after its formal acceptance. Although he never lived to see the second, revised edition in print, let alone the three subsequent editions, Ricketts would have been more than pleased, and perhaps a little surprised, to know that in the world of publishing, *Between Pacific Tides* realized its potential of breaking through.

Intercalary I

Up to this point in their lives, Leopold and Ricketts were, more or less, following high-end, traditional career paths. With the publication of *Game Management,* Leopold invented the discipline of wildlife biology. And with the publication of *Between Pacific Tides,* Ricketts gave the growing West Coast population its first field guide to the Pacific shore.

These accomplishments, by themselves, made both men notable in their time. But had they done these works and nothing else, their legacies most likely would have been as historical figures. As the founder of the discipline, Leopold's name would have been the first mentioned in any modern text on wildlife biology, but most of the techniques he employed and many of the conclusions he drew have since been supplanted by more modern methods and additional data. Ricketts's field guide would have been replaced by more specialized guides with less biology and better color reproduction. Considering the tendencies of people pulling together book projects, many of Leopold's and Ricketts's original ideas would have been lifted without acknowledging the source.

So we can be confident that neither professional book would have made its author the transcendent figure each is today. Instead, what made these men timeless were their second books, *A Sand County Almanac* and *Sea of Cortez,* which broke through the boundaries of traditional science into the realm of personal experience, both theirs and ours. As a result, these books became some-thing every human being could relate to. And what made them enduring were experiences acquired in shacks.

CHAPTER SIX

The Shack

In 1933, when Leopold published *Game Management,* it was well received, especially among scientists, conservationists, and sportsmen. With this book he not only created an entirely new academic discipline, but when, on June 26, 1933, the Wisconsin Alumni Research Foundation approved eight thousand dollars per year for five years to support a game management program, Leopold also finagled the first-ever academic appointment in wildlife biology, at the University of Wisconsin in Madison.[1] The *New York Times* "hailed it as the one and only 'wild game chair.'" [2]

The question—for anybody, not just academics—is, How do you top the big thing you just did, the thing you know you will always be remembered for? At age thirty-three, Alexander the Great is said to have wept when he realized he had no more worlds to conquer. Darwin followed up his *Origin of Species* by working out the pollination biology of orchids. Leopold followed up *Game Management* by putting his ideas into action. He first leased, then bought, eighty acres on the Wisconsin River, just north of Baraboo and east of the Wisconsin Dells. The place had a shack—an old chicken coop—and the property took its name from the building. Leopold and his family began spending weekends there. At the Shack, Leopold did two things. First, he began putting into action the principles outlined in *Game Management.* He planted trees and restored prairie—managing habitat for wildlife. As Stephen Jay Gould has written, "science . . . dedicates itself above all to fruitful doing, not clever thinking; to claims that can be tested by actual research, not to exciting thoughts that inspire no activity."[3] The other thing that Leopold did was to think deeply—beyond science—about game management. With his predawn coffeepot and his notebooks, he was doing more than simply recording bird songs. Many of these thoughts, strung together, became essays, and many of these essays became his second book, *A Sand County Almanac,* which eventually did indeed top everything else that Leopold did. Leopold did not purchase the Shack in order to provide material for his new book (in fact, no new book was planned); however, without the experiences and perspectives accumulated at the Shack, it is doubtful that anything like *A Sand County Almanac* would have been written.

Unlike the purchase of Leopold's Missouri cabin, the acquisition of the Shack is less a story about buying a building than it is one about buying land and happening to find a building. Nina Leopold Bradley wrote in her essay, "A Daughter's Reflections," "In an essay found among my father's works, he had written, 'there are two things that interest me: the relation of people to each other, and the relation of people to land.' As a place to put such ideas to work, my father bought a 'sand farm' in 1935 along the Wisconsin River, first worn out then abandoned by our bigger-and-better society."[4]

As with many things associated with life, there is a separation, a disconnect, between origin and ultimate utility.[5] The wings of the first birds had nothing to do with flying; they were likely thermoregulatory devices that expanded and eventually became modified for flight. And so it was with the purchase of the Shack.[6] During the fall of 1934, two counties in Wisconsin staged the nation's first bow-hunting deer season in a century. Aldo, Estella, Starker, and Luna tracked a dozen bucks through new snow. They shot, and their arrows missed, but they had great fun; so they decided to look for some old farmland to use as a base camp. The land quest continued into the winter. As Meine relates, on January 12, 1935, a day after Leopold's forty-eighth birthday, he and his friend Ed Ochsner drove in and around the Baraboo Hills region, centered in Sauk County, north of Madison.[7] The Baraboo Hills are the weathered but still spectacular quartzite remains of an ancient mountain range. Ochsner knew his way around this landscape, and eventually they came to a bend in the road near the Wisconsin River and turned onto a two-rut track, which had once been the main pioneer wagon route out of Portage. They stopped at a forlorn site along the river, once a farm, now abandoned.

Nina asks, "This land had been 'lived on' and been 'destroyed' by its former owners. If you were selecting a piece of land to purchase, would this be what you would look for?" It was. Leopold leased the place and visited a second time in February. Again Nina:

> Our introduction to Dad's farm came on a winter day in [1935] when he drove his family—his wife and five children and the dog—to have a look at the recently acquired farm. We drove the 50 miles in a February blizzard, shoveling out of snowdrifts and finally trudging

the last quarter mile on foot through the snow. We arrived
to find the only remaining building, an old chicken coop,
complete with chicken perches and waist deep with frozen
manure. As far as the eye could see was corn stubble,
cockleburs, broken fences, and blowing sand and snow.[8]

Leopold visited the Shack for five days in late April (spring
break—a trend that would continue as Leopold's academic calen-
dar and the time for spring tree planting coincided). A week after
this trip he wrote, "Bought place through Ed Ochsner." The price
was eight dollars an acre.[9] Leopold returned to the property once
in May, twice in June, and twice in July. During these early—1935
and 1936—trips he initiated the activities that would characterize
most of the family's trips to the Shack: starting plantings (food
plots and trees), improving the livability of the structure (installing
first a clay floor and later a wooden floor, and nailing batten along
the outside), discovering breeding birds, and noting the phenology
of the native plants (timing of emergence, flowering, seed set, etc.)
and migrating birds.

At the Shack, meals were cooked over a campfire or in a Dutch
oven.[10] There was song, though Leopold was too shy to join in. In
one of the most memorable photographs from the Shack, dating
to about 1937, young Nina arrives toting a picnic basket, some
notebooks, a guitar, and by all accounts what should be a Fox
double-barreled shotgun. At night they slept on straw mattresses.

In late January 1939, the Shack was vandalized by two local
boys. The Leopolds arrived on February 1 to find the place a
mess. The furniture and the dinner plates were destroyed, and
kerosene had been poured over their supply of honey and home-
made preserves. When the initial family reaction was to retreat
and mourn, Leopold smiled and said, "I didn't know how much

this place meant to you. Let's get busy."[11] In the process of cleaning up they made improvements, building a wooden floor over the clay and giving the interior a bright white coat of paint.

At the Shack, Leopold and his children kept a journal. On the unnumbered first page of the first Shack journal (four notebooks were eventually filled, three in his lifetime), Leopold typed,

> The Leopold Shack lies in Secs. 33 & 34, T. 13 N. R 6 E, Sauk County, Wisconsin. 80 acres were purchased in April 1935, and later added to. After 1940 the property comprised 123 acres.
>
> The observations recorded in this journal pertain to this property, and often also the immediately surrounding region south of the Wisconsin River.
>
> The observations and entries were made by Starker, Luna, Nina, and Carl Leopold, by myself, and at times by guests whose names are given. The map used in this volume was drawn by Carl Leopold in 1940.[12]

Entries to the Shack journals were made in pencil. For each entry, visitors to the Shack were written in the top left corner, the date in the top right. Visitors almost always included members of the family, indicated by their initials (AL for Aldo, ASL for Starker, ACL for Carl, EBL for Estella, EEL for Estella Jr., LBL for Luna, NL for Nina) or first name (Estella Jr. was sometimes "little Estella"). Occasionally, "whole family" is written. Extended family also visited; Leopold's mother, Clara, came, as did his brother Frederic. Graduate students spent time there; for example, Fred and Fran Hamerstrom, who were working with Paul Errington at the time, came many times. Art Hawkins's first trip may have been March 19–20, 1937. (Hawkins worked with Leopold from 1935 to 1937, when he received his master's degree.

He went on to have a distinguished career as a waterfowl biologist with the U.S. Fish and Wildlife Service.) Bob McCabe and Joe Hickey, the students who would eventually take over Leopold's position at Wisconsin, were often at the Shack. Leopold took his classes to the Shack on Saturday May 11, 1940, and on May 1, 1943. Colleagues and friends came, including Bill Vogt, Herb Stoddard, and Charles Elton. The journalist and incomparable outdoor writer Gordon MacQuarrie visited the Shack on October 12–13, 1940. Perhaps reflecting a conversation with MacQuarrie, Leopold wrote, "Why do rabbits eat pines so much around the shack and not elsewhere? In winter they get a lot in the woods, but the whites [pines] along the road and in the birchrow are not touched." Sometimes the group at the Shack was identified only as "AL et al." Leopold occasionally went by himself ("AL"), or with his dog ("AL and Flick").

Many journal entries are titled, for example, "SPRING PLANT-ING" or "VACATION." Most journal entries are divided into sections, including "Weather," "Phenology," "Planting," "Work" (which often included planting), "Trees," "Foodpatch," "Garden," "Birds," "Bandings," "Mammals," "River," "Frogs heard," "Fishing," "Hunt-ing," and, in woodcock breeding season, "Peenting." One title, for the November 25–27, 1943, entry detailing the death of their dog, is titled, sadly, "Gus' Last Hunt." Other entries include maps, tables, and graphs of data. The Shack journals are carefully indexed by subject, and the pre-index pages of each journal contain tables, figures, and notes comprising the first analytical cut of the data contained within.

Some interesting trends emerge from an analysis of the dates when the Shack journal indicates the Leopolds visited.[13] On look-ing at the number of days the Shack was occupied (figure 1), it is

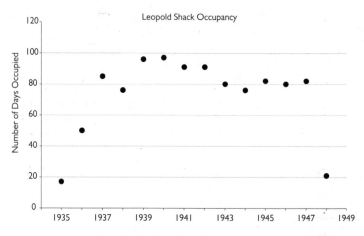

Figure 1. Number of days the Shack was occupied per year, based on the information from the Shack journals. Note the moderate drop-off in days visited during World War II, followed by a slight rebound.

apparent that the Leopolds grew to appreciate their new property. In 1935 they spent only seventeen days at the Shack. In part this was due to Leopold's three-month trip to observe German forestry practices that fall (he left Madison on July 31 and returned in late November); in part this was due to substandard facilities (the Shack was not initially weatherproofed, and the Parthenon [outhouse] was not built until 1936); in part this was due to simply not yet understanding the joy that would come from being there. Nina writes,

> Little enthusiasm was expressed by the family until, on subsequent weekends, we found ourselves involved in fixing up the old chicken coop for weekend living quarters. Materials for repair came not from the lumber yard but from the floodplain of the Wisconsin River,

which bounded the north edge of the farm. I think he got this idea from his reading of Thoreau. Such treasures as old bridge pilings, 2 × 4's, planks of all widths and lengths became crucial material for benches, siding, tabletops, and window frames.

Windows and a door for the Shack my father found in the local dump. Today, I find myself smiling as I contemplate Dad, the sophisticated university professor, scrounging through the dump, looking for usable objects!

Building a fireplace involved the entire family as we hoisted a huge limestone block into place as a lintel. Dad cut a red cedar from the moraine above the Shack, hand-hewn boards from the log, and with a linseed oil finish made a handsome mantle. As carefully engineered as was this fireplace, it smoked in the 1930s and it smokes today. . . .

Mixed with these weekends of hard work was plenty of fun and excitement—censusing woodcock at dusk, singing before the fire at dark, watching the oak coals at night as they warmed our shins. Family camaraderie grew and expanded—never to die.[14]

In 1936 the number of Shack days rose to 50, followed by 85 in 1937, and 76 in 1938. From 1939 to 1942, the family spent more than 90 days annually at the Shack, an average of one day in every four. From 1943 to 1945, World War II took its toll and the number of Shack visits dropped to 80 in 1943, 76 in 1944, and 82 in 1945. Following the war, this reduced level of visits continued, with 80 days in 1946 and 82 days in 1947. Leopold visited the Shack 21 days in 1948 before his death in late April.

Shack visits were not uniformly distributed throughout the year, nor were trip lengths equal. Weeklong trips were made in April. These trips corresponded to the University of Wisconsin's

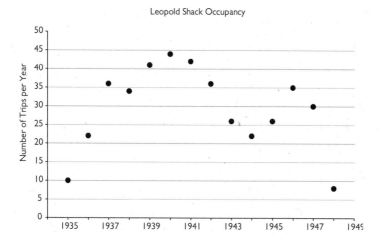

Figure 2.   Number of trips to the Shack per year, based on the information from the Shack journals. Note the steep decline in number of trips (likely a result of gas rationing) and the steep rebound (but not to 1939–41 levels) following the war.

spring break, and their chief purpose was to plant trees. Week-long trips in June constituted real "vacations," at least in name. Weeklong stays in October were hunting trips. Decembers were usually sparse times for recorded Shack visits, and after 1942 there were few recorded January and February trips.[15]

As the children grew up and moved on, their initials drop out of the Shack journals. By 1939, Starker was married and living in Missouri, Luna was at Harvard, and Nina and Carl were undergraduates at the University of Wisconsin.[16] By the fall of 1942, Nina had married Bill Elder and Carl had married Keena Rogers; fifteen-year-old Estella was the only one of the children remaining at home.[17]

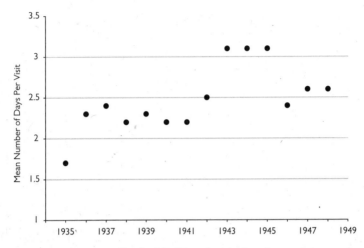

Figure 3.   Days per Shack visit. Note that during the war years, and only during the war years, the average length of each visit rose to more than three days.

World War II influenced the Shack visits. As the plots for number of trips (figure 2) and number of days per trip (figure 3) show, during the heart of World War II the Leopolds took fewer trips to the Shack (fewer than 30 rather than the typical 30 to 45; figure 2), but stayed longer (averaging more than 3 days per trip, rather than the usual 2 to 3). Gas rationing had its effect, although the Leopolds must have saved more coupons than most, with Aldo walking the eight to ten blocks to and from his campus office.[18]

A second trend in Shack visits during the war was only partly due to the conflict. Whereas prewar entries indicated that the children were often there (ASL, ACL, LBL, NL, EEL), wartime entries were often only Aldo, Estella (EBL), and the teenage Estella Jr. (EEL, or "little Estella").[19] Starker is mentioned in several entries from the fall of 1943. And whereas prewar visitors could be anyone, wartime visitors were often couples (Doris and Carl Harper, Joe and Peggy Hickey, Lyle and Greta Sowls). After the war, Aldo combined his Shack and Hunting journals, along with accounts of class field trips to the university's arboretum, a bus trip to Burlington, Iowa (later written up in *A Sand County Almanac* as "Illinois Bus Ride"), and a field trip to Horicon Marsh.

The Shack journals are also noteworthy for what they do not record. There is no mention of family issues or war issues, or even professional issues beyond the data gathered at the Shack. We know Leopold thought deeply while at the Shack, and we know that at times certain issues weighed heavily on his mind. It is a testimony to his determination and focus that no mention of these things creeps into the Shack journals.

On April 21, 1948, the day Leopold died, the first line of the Shack journal entry reads, "4/21 *Weather* clear, calm, cold, frost on grass, 36° at 600 AM. SW wind." The last entry Leopold wrote— likely the last words he wrote—was, "*Bloodroot in Shower Bed* Closed 6 AM."

The next Shack journal entry is three months later, from July 10–11, 1948. Estella, Estella Jr., Nina, and Luna were there. It begins: "Spent Sat aft, & Sunday warm, partly cloudy; calm Saturday; S breeze Sunday[.] work done: Cut most of lawn—very dry, no rain for at least one week."

A year later, on July 2, 1949, in blue pen, Leopold's friends Bill and Marjorie Vogt wrote in page 1 of the fourth Shack journal, "A memorable day at the 'Shack,' rounding out impressions half complete during the years and bridging the gap of the last twelve years. A sad return, yet because life and spirit go on, with the pines, the deer, the pheasants and the butterfly weed, here are still joy and peace, and the knowledge that a great tree will keep on growing, from these deep-sunk roots!"

On the same page, with the same blue pen, Durwood L. Allen wrote, "What Thoreau found at Walden Pond we have found here. We have taken it with us but others will find it undiminished. Never to be forgotten is the shack and the warm friendship it harbors."

CHAPTER SEVEN

The Lab

When Ed Ricketts arrived, the Monterey Peninsula was "still a quiet part of the world, a pleasant end of the road along one of the loveliest of seashores . . . not as different in 1923 from what Sebastian Viscaino had seen in 1602 as it is now."[1] As Bruce Ariss colorfully describes it, Monterey Peninsula is heavily wooded, surprisingly small, and roughly circular. From Huckleberry Hill, looking only five miles in every direction, you can see the whole of its irregular and spectacular coastline. In an airplane "it looks like a bear's head jutting out into the sea. Carmel is on the back of its neck, the two ears are at Pescadero Point in Pebble Beach and at Cypress Point. To the north its nose supports a sparkling lighthouse at Point Piños. Pacific Grove is in the bear's mouth, Cannery Row lies under its jaw, and Monterey, the largest of the three towns, spreads out along its throat and chest."[2] Aside from churches, in 1923 the principal intellectual establishment of the peninsula was the Hopkins Marine Station of Stanford University, recently relocated to Cabrillo Point, not far from the canneries.

Galigher and Ricketts's original laboratory was a "ware-house like building" on 165 Fountain Avenue in Pacific Grove, across the street from Holman's store.[3] After only a year in business together, Galigher and Ricketts dissolved their partnership (Hedgpeth says it was because both were pursuing the same woman) and Galigher took the microscope slide preparation business (which Ricketts later reestablished) with him to Berkeley.[4]

Ed became the sole owner of Pacific Biological Laboratories, and in 1928, after the space he was renting was sold,[5] he moved the business to a small, two-story waterfront building sandwiched between the Del Vista Packing Company and the Del Mar Canning Company[6] at 740 Ocean View Avenue (the address was later renumbered 800) in neighboring New Monterey.[7] In his notes from a shareholder's meeting at the time he wrote, "[The] only desirable possibility was a location backing the waterfront in new Monterey, on Oceanview Avenue, a paved street. It consists of a 50' lot with a stoutly built three-bedroom plastered house in fair condition and a cement-floored shed in fair shape containing four cement tanks offering a splendid place for storing dogfish (heretofore a serious problem). This property was priced at $8000, $1000 down."[8] Rodger continues, "By the fall of 1928, Ricketts was comfortably settled into his new Lab sandwiched between two canneries."[9]

"During this time, when the sardines were being processed Cannery Row was excitement, noise, and raw vitality."[10] It was also noxious. A stench that only fish rendering can produce "would waft all the way to sunbathers at the posh Hotel Del Monte in Old Monterey almost a mile away."[11] Ariss relates, "in the height of the sardine season the smell of burning fish was awful—overwhelming, almost unbearable. The coarse yellow smoke from the [cannery] retorts and chimneys curled along the street, gagging the passersby who hurried along with handkerchiefs held to their noses." He elaborates: "The horrifying aroma in those days gave rise to a very popular description of the Monterey Peninsula's three small cities: the town full of tourists, art galleries, and gift shops was Carmel-by-the Sea, the town full of churches and quaint Victorian cottages was Pacific Grove-by-God, and the sardine packing town was Monterey-by-the-Smell."[12] Odors never seemed to bother Ed Ricketts. According to Ariss, "we often visited Ed Ricketts in the bay side yard of his laboratory, where he distilled shark liver oil, boiling it down to a syrup that was dark brown and nasty smelling. He sold it for a pet food additive, but drank it religiously himself."[13]

Pacific Biological Laboratories has been described by Steinbeck and Benson as follows: It is a low building facing the street that had been built as a small, one-bedroom house over a basement-garage. There is a stairway up the front of the building to the front door. The front door leads to an entry hall, which Ed had turned into an office. Crammed into this small space were a roll-top desk piled high with unopened mail, filing cabinets, and a safe, which was used for keeping cheese and canned sardines. Around the walls were shelves, which held dusty jars of specimens offered for sale by the Lab. To the left of the office, also in the front of the house, was what had been the living room, now a combination bedroom for Ed (he moved in after his wife left him) and gathering place. This room Steinbeck called the library or music room, and writes, "The walls are bookcases to the ceiling, boxes of pamphlets and separates, books of all kinds, dictionaries, encyclopedias, poetry, plays." Ricketts's phonograph was in this room, and beside it, lined up, were hundreds of records reflecting his eclectic tastes. Steinbeck continues, "Under the window is a redwood bed and on the walls to the bookcases are pinned reproductions of Daumiers, and Graham, Titian, and Leonardo and Picasso, Dali and George Grosz, pinned here and there at eye level so that you can look at them if you want to. There are chairs and benches in this little room and of course the bed. As many as forty people have been in here at one time."[14]

Ariss adds, "The Lab was heated by an old gas floor furnace that Ed turned on with a key. The pilot was sparked by two Model T Ford coils, rigged up by Paul Verbeck [the Belgian who also built Ricketts's phonograph], which made a buzzing sound like a rattlesnake before the gas was ignited."[15]

When Ed Jr. was not living with Ricketts, the former kitchen, in the rear of the house, became a slide-preparation room, with microscopes, trays, slides, glassware, and chemicals. Steinbeck describes this room as "a narrow chamber with a gas stove, a water heater, and a sink. But whereas some food is kept in the filing cabinets in the office, dishes and cooking fat and vegetables are kept in glass-fronted sectional bookcases in the kitchen. No whimsy dictated this. It just happened. From the ceiling of the kitchen hang pieces of bacon, and salami, and black bêche-demur." Behind the kitchen [in the postfire Lab] were the Lab's toilet and a shower. Steinbeck notes, "The toilet leaked for five years until a clever and handsome guest fixed it with a piece of chewing gum."

Steinbeck describes the room behind the office, which was the laboratory, the heart of the business: "In aquaria are many living animals; there are also the microscopes and the slides and the drug cabinets, the cases of laboratory glass, the work benches and little motors, the chemicals." Biology is a smelly business, as Steinbeck notes: "From this room come smells—formaline, and dry starfish, and sea water and menthol, carbolic acid and acetic acid, smell of brown wrapping paper and straw and rope, smell of chloroform and ether, smell of ozone from the motors, smell of fine steel and thin lubricant from the microscopes, smell of banana oil and rubber tubing, smell of drying wool socks and boots, [the] sharp pungent smell of rattlesnakes, and [the] musty frightening smell of rats." And through the back door came the antidote, the "smell of salt and spray when the tide is in."

Because the building had once been raised and the garage and basement put underneath, there were no stairs inside the Lab; they were outside in both the front and the back. The basement was where the business of the Lab interfaced with the world. Here the animals were prepared, packed, and shipped. Steinbeck writes, "The basement is a storeroom with shelves, shelves clear to the ceiling loaded with jars of preserved animals. And in the basement is a sink and instruments for embalming and for injecting." Behind the Lab was "a covered shed on piles over the ocean and here are the tanks for the larger animals, the sharks and rays and octopi, each in their concrete tanks."

Benson adds, "When Ed moved into the house to live as well as work there, he simply added a bed he made himself, a sort of nautical bunk made of a redwood frame crosshatched with rope, and put some food in the former kitchen."

For those who think of the Lab with Ricketts and Steinbeck in it, talking and laughing, conversations quick and clever, with their young, smart "termite" artist friends, swilling quart beers and cheap wine, the following description by Benson seems a little too clinical: "Inside, the Lab . . . was rather dark, battered, and lacking color. Masculine, shopworn, with clutter all around." Then we remember Steinbeck's words in *Travels with Charley,* "I discovered a long time ago in collecting and classifying marine animals that what I found was closely intermeshed with how I felt at the moment. External reality has a way of not being so external after all."[16] We can wonder why Benson was in such a bad mood.

During the spring and summer of 1932, Carol Steinbeck was also in the Lab quite a lot, working part-time for Ed. Steinbeck wrote to his friend George Albee, "Carol is working now and she loves it. She has two rattlesnakes and about 200 white rats to love." In a letter to Albee later that summer, he wrote, "Carol lost her job . . . because Ed could no longer afford to pay her." As Steinbeck explained, "Ed's wife just left him taking all the available money and leaving lots of debts . . . we'll feed him until he has money. He is a very good man. His wife left him because he was interested in things other than bridge and kiddies."[17]

In late 1936, Cannery Row caught fire and Ricketts's Lab was incinerated. Steinbeck writes, "One night something went wrong with the electric current on the whole waterfront. Where 220 volts were expected and prepared for, something like two thousand volts came through. Since in the subsequent suits the electric company was found blameless by the courts, this must be set down to an act of God."[18] Perhaps the best description of Ricketts and the Cannery Row fire comes from Eric Tamm. On November 25, about 5:30, Ricketts awoke, "feeling 'impressed with a sense of stillness but with the notion that something was wrong.' He looked out the front window of the lab and then went to the door. He saw three men standing in the quiet street, their faces awash in a glow of dancing light. Flames were leaping out of the Del Mar Cannery next door. Ricketts could hear the crackling of the fire." He panicked, pulled on a few clothes, and "rushed downstairs to get his car out of the garage. He reversed the car, stopping at the staircase of the second story entry. He jumped out and rushed upstairs to grab a painting. By the time he made a second dash inside, the power poles were ablaze and the lights had gone out in the lab. He found a flashlight and searched for two books of records, then quickly left." The Lab did not offer much resistance to the conflagration. "Within eight to ten minutes the entire lab was a sheet of fire. . . . In three hours, only ash and char and popping sardine cans remained where Ricketts' lab and the cannery once stood. . . . His entire life's work [including his precious and valuable library] had literally gone up in smoke."[19]

When Bruce and Jean Ariss returned to Monterey the following evening, they described the scene in terms of war. "It looked like it had been blitzed. Smoking hills of charred timbers writhed amongst smelly mountains of burned sardine cans in every direction. Occasionally, an overheated can in one of the steaming mounds would explode like a small bomb and pop ten or fifteen feet up into the air." And they noted that despite narrowly escaping with his life, Ricketts viewed the incident more philosophically than in terms of personal loss—life went on. About the losses, they wrote, "Everyone did what they could for Ed. Clothes, books, and records were collected for him. John swung a loan for rebuilding. Remo drew the plans and the carpenters tried to restore the Lab, as much as possible, just as it had been before the fire."[20]

While rebuilding the Lab, Ricketts stayed with his sister and brother-in-law, Frances and Fred Strong. On December 16, he wrote to V. E. Bogard and Austin Flanders, "We have the lot almost entirely cleaned up, still one large pile of wood and debris staked together. Most of the concrete seems to be alright." He continued, "Rough plans have been drawn for a shack-like board and bat structure to house office and labs, 28 × 33'. Estimated cost, top $981, plus $100 for rough plumbing and $75 for conduit, or vice versa. Labor and material plus 5%. Estimates by builder who does much of the cannery work and who was sent up into Oregon by 3 of the local canneries to build 5 plants there." By necessity, Ricketts recycled: "We have saved lots of conduit, cast iron pipe (all of which is good), and some valves and galvanized pipe that seems alright; this will reduce the cost. Galv. Iron too expensive."[21]

By the end of January 1937, a new Lab was built. Ricketts liked the arrangement of the original building so much that he had it rebuilt with exactly the same floor plan.[22] The building was "a glorified shanty, but a structurally sound one; the building stood for sixty years before it underwent a restoration and seismic retrofit in the 1990s, which won the California Governor's Award for Historic Preservation."[23]

On February 8, 1937, Ricketts wrote to his brother and sister-in-law, Thayer and Evelyn Ricketts, "Looks as tho the firm [Pacific Biological] will be able to pull out of this, and I also. But it's a great strain. I have not only more work than I can hope to do, but much more than even an efficient person could figure on doing." About the cost, he wrote that the total actual "loss must be more than $12,000; and there was only $3,000 insurance! Then there were a thousand and one little personal things that I hated to lose. A good many were superfluous, but some are essential to proper conduct of the business and/or my comfort. If everything is going along after a year more, we shall have survived, but it will be a struggle." He had, however, turned a corner. "I'm staying [at the Lab] now. It's pretty comfortable. A Franklin stove (fireplace type) went in this afternoon, and there is a floor furnace . . . shower, bath, gas stove." There was also an upgrade, an "indoor toilet—a luxury not possible before." He summarizes, "I have a really nice apartment, and an extra room was built that can be used as a spare lab or as a spare bedroom. All board and bat construction, but my room and the office have been insulated with 3 ply and celotex and are really pretty comfortable."[24]

On the same date he wrote to Howard and Emma Flanders, distant relatives, "The lab is pretty well put back together. I was surprised to see how much could be done with a little money, some common sense, and a bit of accumulated experience. Some, at least, of the previous errors weren't reenacted." And about the rebuilding process, he wrote, "Funny, tho, how hard it is to start out. I'd (almost literally) reach for a sheet of paper, or for a well accustomed reference, only to find out that it no longer existed, and that even the place where it stood was gone. Imagine me (at first) prowling around, cold and wanting hot coffee; no shoes or sox, or coat. There was no point of reference aside from a blazing heap of ashes and a car."[25]

He also wrote to Austin and Hazel Flanders about the rebuilding process. "The notion of starting with a cheap shack was a good idea. That was the first light I saw in a complicated situation. If I had started out with the idea of trying to put up a good building, hung between cement walls, as I would have liked to do, it would have been impossible right from the start. As it is, a pretty good building eventuated." To raise money he traded in his Packard for a Ford. "A funny little car. V-8 60 h.p. Smallest standard car built I imagine. I don't like it very well, but it will provide cheap transportation." And then Ricketts justified his decision. "I presume there will never be so long cost per ton-hour-mile as in that old Packard, but now I am trying to avoid both the miles and the tons. Since there is no longer a big family to cart around on long collecting trips, nor for that matter, not even the possibility of very long or time-consuming trip, this should be easy."[26]

It took another year for Ricketts to get a new phonograph. On February 21, 1938, he wrote to watercolor painter Jim Fitzgerald, "I now have a phonograph and radio receiver built by Pol Verbeck, who made Dick Albee's and John's fine sets. This is the best so far." In the same letter, he wrote, "And we have been cold, in single board, cracked houses."[27]

A few weeks later, March 4, Ricketts wrote to Dick Albee about his phonograph and other things: "Pol hit the nail on the head; says I have a queer and secretive business with that-there-now science, that the seat of the business is located in a queer and out of the way place. That I am queer. And worst of all, I have books on magic, and medieval philosophy, and bibles, and I play Gregorian music and phonograph pieces with queer time patterns that make not only my windows rattle but Flora's as well." Then Ricketts, perhaps distracted by thoughts of Flora's business—the brothel across the street—offers an off-color, stream-of-consciousness riff before getting back to his main point. "And if the gals over there can't rattle the windows in the pursuit of their no-doubt pleasant business—did I say pleasant or oh I was thinking of the peasant-pheasant confusion—no one can. But I do. So that proves it. I was thinking originally about my beautiful new machine [phonograph]. And it's as good as it's beautiful."[28]

Following the release of Steinbeck's *Cannery Row* in 1945, *Time* magazine reporter Bob de Roos and *Life* magazine photographer Peter Stackpole visited the district.[29] In an interview with Martha Heasley Cox in 1975, Stackpole recalled, "We ran into Ed Ricketts, who was a close friend [of Steinbeck's]. Ricketts was quite friendly with us and allowed us the run of his house. We photographed him at work and down in the basement and in his lab where he was doing various experiments with sharks and various fishes—which he was doing in the laboratories." About Ricketts's daily life Stackpole wrote, "I remember he had music going all the time. He was very partial to Gregorian Chants."[30]

Ricketts let de Roos shadow him during a trip to the Great Tide Pool at the tip of the Monterey Peninsula. Afterward de Roos wrote, "Ed Ricketts has the best eyes I have ever seen at work. He would sneak up on a tide pool which I swore was absolutely empty of life and point out dozens of nearly invisible transparent creatures." Meeting Ricketts made a deep impression on de Roos. "Doc and I talked for hours but I cannot remember what we talked about. He was a magnetic man, very easy to like, very hard to forget. I have Steinbeck to thank for that meeting."[31]

According to Ariss, both before and after the fire "Ed Ricketts' biological business . . . was often aided by his large coterie of friends, mostly unemployed young artists and writers, who were attracted to his gentle and thoughtful manner and the coffee-house conviviality of his waterfront laboratory. It had become a sort of Depression day social club."[32] Benson writes, "there was always someone stopping by the Lab. The gatherings were irregular and impromptu—no one was sure who would show up or when." And he continues, "Sometimes there were three or four people sitting around the office or in the living room–bedroom, relaxing on a late afternoon: Ed sitting crosslegged on his bed, nursing a quart bottle of beer; John leaning back in the swivel chair, one foot on a packing case; and Ritchie Lovejoy hunched over the back of a straight chair, squinting through the smoke of roll-your-own cigarettes."[33] A few more people—often Carol

[Steinbeck], Tal Lovejoy, Bruce and Jean Ariss—might show up later and throw together a meal. If more people stopped in, the gathering would become a party. Now and then there were planned parties. These often lasted until dawn, and on a few, legendary occasions, for several days.

Benson notes that in the early days of the Lab, "much of the informality, people dropping in and leaving, came from the fact that no one had a telephone and hardly anybody had a car. If something was planned, it might be talked about for days until the word got around—and sometimes the word got around too well." These occasions were reasonably well planned. "For an anticipated event, everyone chipped in what food and drink they could. The wives would bring their little balsa wood cigar boxes with cigarette makings inside, papers and Bull Durham." The attendees were vibrant, dynamic people who had some connection with the arts. Almost all were political liberals, several were socialists. However, politics and social issues were seldom discussed at the Lab. According to Benson, these were not issues Ricketts cared about, and he tended to be the "mediator and moderator of discussion at the Lab."[34]

Benson also notes that during these gatherings there was music; the songs "played on Ed's phonograph, many songs sung . . . John in his deep voice sang the melody an octave lower than those who carried it, and while Ed couldn't carry a tune, he could harmonize." There was also much "poetry and prose" read out loud. This was a time without television, and many in the group had little money. Instead, there was a "constant enthusiasm for inventing games, trying out activities. There could be almost anything, from automatic writing or a séance, to group composition of dirty limericks, or a costume party that parodied the dress and affectations of the wealthy." When Joseph Campbell was there he remembers they had 'Let's get together and read a book parties.' Someone would check out a new novel from the library, or dig out an old classic, and everyone would sit around and take turns reading aloud from the book until late into the night. Reflecting the group's wide interests, the books read and talked about during these years varied widely. Benson cites a range of works, from the "essays of Jung, to poems by Jeffers, the latest Huxley novel, or stories by Saroyan." And according to Benson, "Virginia Scardigli remembers the atmosphere of the Lab as 'Let's dig, let's find out'—a spirit which was in large part generated by the presence of Ed." It was at the Lab where Ricketts and Steinbeck, with the help of their friends, worked out the ideas presented in *Sea of Cortez.*

In contrast to the family and friends that gathered at Leopold's Shack, Ricketts's Lab was, in the words of Benson, a kaleidoscope, which everyone who was there remembered it slightly differently, probably because it was different at different times. Gatherings at the Lab gained their "character from the number and kinds of people who happened to come together, and the number and kinds of people shifted from day to day, week to week, and year to year." Benson continues, "At its best (from a literary or artistic point of view), the Lab could be an exciting place full of conversation, experiment, and discovery. . . . One could turn the kaleidoscope and see in the Lab a collection of sages and explorers, artists and philosophers spinning in their orbits of curiosity and enthusiasm about the nucleus of Ed Ricketts's acceptance." But "Turn the kaleidoscope again and the Lab might resemble nothing so much as a neighborhood bar, a place for people who were too poor to go anyplace else to get together to drink and talk, joke and tell stories, and sing."[35] There was one rule: the Lab crowd "did not much care for the person who came there carrying his talent on his back . . . no one should, in the evening, get too serious about what he was doing during the day. If one spoke about his work at all, it must be self-deprecating and in jest."[36]

Ricketts's financial situation always seemed to be the opposite of the country's. During the Depression, when the country struggled, he had some money; his Lab was the "bank." During World War II and after, as the country prospered, Ricketts foundered. On March 16, 1942, he wrote to his daughter, Nancy Jane,

> I have still the same car. Now 5 years old and never wonderful at that. A pity I couldn't have got a new one before the priorities went in, but with care, I can get by. I have to be careful of money, more careful than ever before. Most people, especially you people, are earning more money than ever before, but I am earning less, and I think it's a chronic condition with me, and don't worry about it much anymore. I do some significant work, there are 2 good books that I largely had a hand in, and I do a lot of other (I think) significant things thru influencing and catalyzing. Or so I think. But for bringing home the bacon I was never very hot, and I'm getting less so. Which is alright too. There are lots of different kinds of work to be done in the world, and some of that is thankless and profitless, but nevertheless to be done.[37]

And in 1943, Ricketts wrote to Calvin, "So, PBL is going to pieces in its own amiable way," although it continued to serve as combination home and lab for Ed and coffeehouse-bar for his friends.[38] The paradox of Ricketts's life at this time was that, while Steinbeck's *Cannery Row* had made him famous, Pacific Biological Laboratories could not rebound from the wartime economy to the point that it could sustain the lifestyle Steinbeck had celebrated. Ricketts went to work as a chemist for the California Packing Corporation.[39]

After Ricketts died, Steinbeck wrote from New York to his longtime friend and lawyer, Webster F. (Toby) Street in Monterey, "Now there is something else that I want you to look into. I loaned Ed a thousand dollars very recently. I have his correspondence on it and he was to have signed a note for it as he indicates in his letters. This thousand was to be his share of the expenses for the book we were going to do together. That I will have to get back somehow. He may have spent it on other things. I know he was pretty strapped and that his beer bill alone was more than he was making."[40]

Intercalary II

Leopold's Shack and Ricketts's Lab provided the settings for these men to transcend their professional philosophies and move into the realm of common experience. These are the places where we celebrate the spirit of the two men.

Leopold's Shack allowed him to be close to the environments he loved. It allowed him to observe, study, and engage with the natural world. Further, because Leopold was a solitary thinker, the Shack offered time for contemplation. Not only did the Shack experiences furnish him with much of the material for *A Sand County Almanac,* the place itself gave him the time to work through his science until it became literature. It was at the Shack that Leopold's "Land Ethic" was able to emerge.

Ricketts's Lab was also close to nature—his beloved tide pools— but perhaps more than that it became a gathering place for his wide variety of friends, the talented and beautiful writers, artists, musicians, and craftsmen of quirky early Monterey (including John and Carol Steinbeck, Joseph Campbell, John Cage, Toni Jackson, and Bruce and Jean Ariss). It was with these friends, through discourse sometimes highbrow and sometimes lowbrow, that Ricketts worked out his worldview of "breaking through." As we will see, when Ricketts and Steinbeck went into the Sea of Cortés, their boat, the *Western Flyer,* was nothing so much as a floating extension of Ricketts's Lab.

These days, people wanting to experience the spirit of Leopold and Ricketts do not just read their works, or read the words written about them; they go to their buildings. They touch and smell and see. At the Shack it becomes possible to experience the natural forces underlying the Land Ethic, and at the Lab it is possible to imagine yourself "breaking through" to a place of inclusiveness you did not know to be possible.

CHAPTER EIGHT

A Sand County Almanac

In early July 1941, Leopold flew to the Delta Waterfowl Station in Manitoba, Canada, where he conferred with his former student and station director, Al Hochbaum. As Meine details, Leopold and Hochbaum had for some time spoken informally about working together on a book of essays.[1] Leopold was to provide the text, Hochbaum the drawings. By August 1941, plans for the book had become more definite, though the two men set no firm schedule. That fall, Leopold began crafting the first essays, drawing from his Shack experiences.[2]

About the same time, Harold Strauss, an editor at Knopf, approached Leopold about pulling together "a good book on wildlife observations . . . a personal book recounting adventures in the field." Leopold turned the project down but offered that he was "focusing my effort on a series of ecological essays, illustrated, as a Christmas book for next year. The M.S. is well along. Are you interested by any chance?" Meine says, "Strauss replied that he was 'emphatically interested' . . . so much interested that I am not inclined to wait until the manuscript is altogether finished. Won't you send me whatever material is in shape?"[3]

By April 1943, nearly eighteen months had passed since Leopold had corresponded with Strauss about the essay book. Strauss was in the army and his successor, J. R. de la Torre Bueno, said to Leopold he would be "very happy to hear from you about your work whenever you have anything to say."[4]

As Leopold completed essays he would send them to Hochbaum. During the first half of 1944 they corresponded extensively. As Meine describes it, Hochbaum was a direct and honest critic, and Leopold responded quickly and openly to his sometimes personal suggestions. Both seemed to enjoy this literary give-and-take, which "would alter not only the flavor of Leopold's essays, but also the process of self examination that went into them."[5]

Considering the essays as a whole, Hochbaum wrote, "In many of these you seem to follow one formula: you paint a beautiful picture of something that was—a bear, crane, or a parcel of wilderness—then in a word or an epilogue, you, sitting more or less aside as a sage, deplore the fact that brute man has spoiled the things you love. This is never tiresome, and it drives your point deep." Then Hochbaum expressed his biggest concern, "Still, you never drop a hint that you yourself have once despoiled or at least had a strong hand in it. In your writings of the day, you played a hand in influencing the policies, for your case against the wolf was as strong then as for wilderness now. I just read they killed the last lobo in Montana last year. I think you'll have to admit you've got at least a drop of its blood on your hands." Hochbaum then gives appropriate perspective to the situation: "You already sit in a circle which may never hold more than a dozen in the century. What you thought 20 years ago has small part in your influence.

Still, I think your case for wilderness is all the stronger if, in one of these pieces, you admit that you haven't always smoked the same tobacco."[6] Leopold responded, though not initially, and not without some pushback, by penning, on April 1, 1944, one of his classic essays, "Thinking like a Mountain." [7]

That spring, while attending the Ninth North American Wildlife Conference in Chicago, Leopold met Wellmer Pessels, the editor of outdoor books for Macmillan. Like Strauss from Knopf, she expressed an interest and asked him to send her what he had. That summer, according to Meine, Leopold arranged his thirteen essays in the following order: "Marshland Elegy,"* "Song of the Gavilan,"* "Guacamaja," "Escudilla," "Smokey Gold," "Odyssey,"* "Draba," "Great Possessions," "The Green Lagoons,"* "Illinois Bus Ride," "Pines above the Snow,"* "Thinking like a Mountain," and "The Geese Return."[8] Five (asterisked above) had been published before. Leopold called the collection *Thinking like a Mountain—and Other Essays.* On June 6, 1944 (D-day), he sent his essays and Hochbaum's drawings to Macmillan. A month later, Pessels wrote back to say ("with real regret") that although she thought they were "beautiful . . . we do not feel that we can make you a publishing offer." As Meine writes, "She explained that essays always sold modestly, and that wartime paper allotments forced them to choose their new projects carefully. 'I personally regret very much that I shall not have the privilege of working on this book with you.'"[9] Leopold was unperturbed, and inquired into the possibility of personally underwriting publishing costs, as he had done for *Game Management.* She could offer him no encouragement.

About six weeks later, on July 24, Clinton Simpson, Knopf's editor, wrote back with interest and numerous helpful suggestions. He indicated to Leopold that he was "impressed with your writing, with the freshness of observation which it reflects, and the skill of phrase. We believe that readers who like nature will enjoy such writing and hope that we can work out with you a successful plan for a volume." Among the criticisms were comments similar to Hochbaum's, including that the essays "were too scattered in subject matter and too varied in length, writing style, and point of view." Simpson further suggested, "Some sort of unifying theme or principle must be found for a book of this sort, we think, and perhaps it would hold together better if it were limited to a single part of the country." And finally, "Sometimes it seems that you want more intelligent planning, but you point out that nature's balance was upset with the coming of civilization, and you certainly do not seem to like the ordinary band of conservationists and government planners. I think the average reader would be left somewhat uncertain as to what you propose. Perhaps in a single essay, all these ideas could be related so that your basic theme would become clearer."[10] One solution presented itself; in November 1944, Hochbaum and Leopold discussed an almanac format for the book.

In January 1946, Leopold sent the book to the University of Minnesota Press. Two weeks later it was rejected.

In April 1946, Simpson wrote to Leopold asking him about his progress. And although Leopold had been thinking about the book, his time spent teaching kept him from writing. He sent two philosophical essays, which Simpson liked but could not see how to combine them easily with the descriptive essays he had sent previously, or with an almanac format. Simpson wrote, "We certainly have no objection to 'philosophical' writing, when it is as good as this, but I wonder if the subjects of the other pieces are going to fit in with what you have? Or do they group naturally together, so that the book might be organized in two parts, one descriptive and the other philosophical?" And he offered encouragement. "I find whatever you write full of interest and vitality, and it seems to me our only problem is one of fitting together the pieces in a way that will not seem haphazard or annoying to the reader."[11]

Leopold agreed with Simpson's assessment, writing, "I can see no easy way of generating unity between the philosophical essays and the descriptive essays." Meine adds, "It was the same old problem: how to tie the diverse essays together. Only now, by adding his philosophical articles, Leopold was making the collection even more varied. Previously, they had differed in style and geographical setting. Now they varied by level of abstraction."[12]

In February 1947, Albert Hochbaum withdrew from the project because of his responsibilities at the Delta Waterfowl Station. During July, Leopold returned to the book. He had decided to divide it into three sections. The first, titled "A Sauk County Almanac," consisted of essays about his Shack experiences in an almanac format (i.e., cleverly arranged by month). The second, called "Sketches Here and There," consisted of essays from other regions of the Midwest, West, Canada, and Mexico. The third, "The Upshot," contained the philosophical essays. About this time, he combined three previous essays—"The Conservation Ethic" from 1933, "A Biotic View of the Land" from 1939, and his recently published "The Ecological Conscience"—into a new essay that he called "The Land Ethic."[13]

For the rest of the summer he worked on the book, editing

and rewriting the essays to tighten the fit. On September 5 he wrote to Simpson that the book was ready for review, not quite complete but together enough to present "an overall view of the job." On September 11, 1947, he submitted the book, titled *Great Possessions*. Three days later Leopold met with Charles Schwartz in Saint Louis to discuss illustrating the book.[14]

On November 5, Simpson wrote back to Leopold that after three readings the publishers at Knopf had concluded that it was "far from being satisfactorily organized as a book." They wanted Leopold to make the book a simple narrative of life at the Shack, giving it "a natural continuity that the present book lacks."[15] According to Meine, Leopold was "upset and disappointed with the rejection, and especially with the reasons given. He was incensed that they could have failed to appreciate the time he put into the essays; to suggest that he sit down and completely rewrite it was incredible."[16] Leopold was still angry when he talked to Luna, and was beginning to think he might give up on publishing companies altogether and bring out the book himself. Luna had another idea. He told his father, "'You're just too soft-hearted to deal with these people. Put the publication in my hands.' 'Fine,' Aldo answered. 'I'd love it. Get me off the hook.'"[17]

Schwartz was notified of the rejection, with the hope that despite this setback he would continue collaborating. He would, and wrote back that his "enthusiasm hadn't dwindled a bit." Buoyed by the support, Leopold crafted a new essay, "Axe in Hand." Meanwhile, Luna had talked with Philip Vaudrin, a trade editor at Oxford University Press. Vaudrin wrote to Aldo expressing interest "toward making you an offer of publication." Leopold also sent the manuscript to William Sloane Associates, the group publishing his friend Bill Vogt's book, *Road to Survival*.

On the morning of Wednesday, April 14, 1948, Vaudrin called to inform Leopold that Oxford wished to publish his book, if he would be willing to spend the summer making revisions in order for it to be ready for a fall 1949 publication. Vaudrin later wrote, "we are all extremely pleased by the prospect of publishing this book for you." As Meine writes, "Leopold was overjoyed, obviously gratified, and he accepted the offer." Leopold notified Sloane, who wrote back, "Well, it's our own fault; I think we've lost a good book, but fortunately to a good publisher."[18] The next day Leopold and Vaudrin closed the deal and Leopold wired the good news to Schwartz.

The following day, Friday, Leopold wrote the news about *Great Possessions* to Luna, thanking him for his role in brokering the deal. In the afternoon, Leopold, Estella, Estella Jr. (who was now 21), and a boy friend left for what would be Leopold's last visit to the Shack.[19] His death on Wednesday, April 21, cast much doubt on the fate of *Great Possessions*. But just after Leopold and Vaudrin reached their publication agreement, Leopold had penned a letter to some of his most trusted friends—including Fred and Fran Hamerstrom, Bill Vogt, Joe Hickey, and Bob McCabe—asking them to review the book. He wrote, "What I need, of course, is the most critical attitude you are able to muster. Which are the weak ones? What is ambiguous, obscure, repetitious, inaccurate, fatuous, highbrow?"[20]

Leopold died before he had the opportunity to send this note Soon after, Hickey and McCabe discussed the book. Hickey knew the publishing business and wrote a letter to the Leopold family and to the people Aldo identified as readers, telling them, "We must close our ranks and get this book into print."[21] Hickey also wrote to Vaudrin saying that Leopold had been working on the manuscript, that it was in nearly publishable form, and that they would be delivering it within six months. Meine writes that Hickey became the liaison between Oxford, the readers, and the Leopold family; Luna became chief editor; Vogt met with Vaudrin to ensure confidence; and Schwartz finalized the figures.

The readers suggested minor revisions but were reluctant to make substantive changes. The Hamerstroms wrote, "This is a beautiful thing. Better to leave in a few things that might perhaps have been said differently than to risk taking liberties (no matter how well intended) with Aldo's own way of expressing things." In the end, Meine writes, Luna made a handful of major changes in the manuscript, shifted the order of a couple essays, renamed two, and changed the title of the first section to "A Sand County Almanac."[22]

That summer, Vaudrin asked Luna to explore alternative titles. *Great Possessions* was vague, and besides sounded too much like Charles Dickens's famous book. After mulling over the many suggestions offered by Vaudrin and the readers, Luna reluctantly agreed to *A Sand County Almanac,* and the book appeared, on time, in the fall of 1949 with the full title *A Sand County Almanac and Sketches Here and There.*[23]

As Nina wrote in 1987,

> Concern for my father's influence on the general public was farthest from my mind as dad sent us early drafts (on yellow paper) of the individual essays for "A Sand County Almanac." My personal reaction at that time was that the essays must have been written personally for us—for Mother and Dad's children! The thought of outside response did not actually occur to me until the volume reached the book shelves after Dad's death.

For 20 years after publication of the book (1948 *[sic]*–1968),
Dad's audience grew. During the second 20 years (1968–
present), his audience expanded exponentially. Now, as
the book is apparently being read by philosophers and
"men of the cloth," Dad has reached a new and desired
audience.[24]

CHAPTER NINE

Sea of Cortez

In the spring of 1939, Ricketts's *Between Pacific Tides* and Stein-beck's *Grapes of Wrath* were published.[1] Steinbeck was getting a lot of unwanted publicity, especially from conservative politicians and groups such as the Associated Farmers. He was shaken by assertions that he had exaggerated the plight of the Okies, and by being ostracized by Californians, especially former friends (except, of course, for Ed). On October 16, 1939, Steinbeck wrote, "Now I am battered with uncertainties. That part of my life that made the 'Grapes' is over." He sought a solution: "I have one little job to do for the government, and then I can be born again. Must be. I have to go to new sources and find new roots. I have written simply for simple stories, but now the conception and the execu-tion become difficult and not simple." And he thought the solu-tion might lie with his friend, Ed. "I don't quite know what the conception is. But I know it will be found in the tide pools and the microscope slide rather than in men."[2]

During the fall and winter of 1939–40, Steinbeck spent a lot of time in the Lab helping Ricketts, learning marine biology, and preparing for field trips.[3] Ed Jr. recalls, "He was like a kid. Once he and I were trying to figure out how to preserve anemones that Dad kept in tanks in the lab. We got his car and went to buy dry ice thinking we could quick freeze them. We dropped the ice in the tanks not knowing what to expect . . . Then dad came in wondering what was going on; the carbon dioxide was choking him."[4] Ricketts and Steinbeck decided to collaborate on a pair of projects. The first arose from a request by Stanford University Press that Ricketts write a book on San Francisco Bay invertebrates. And Steinbeck had been considering a trip to Mexico, which morphed into the second project, a collecting expedition in the Sea of Cortés (Gulf of California).

In a letter to his agent, Elizabeth Otis, Steinbeck wrote, "Now—the collecting. I got a truck and we are equipping it. We don't go to Mexico until March, but we have the [San Francisco Bay] handbook to do first and we'll go north in about a week I guess for the solstice tides. It will be a tough job and I'm not at all sure we can get it done by March. And I have a terrific job of reading to do." In Steinbeck's mind, the San Francisco Bay handbook would be a start. It would give him credibility and build trust in the minds of biologists. But already he knew the more important project: "The Mexican book will be interesting to a much larger audience, and there is no question that [his publisher] Viking can have it."

Steinbeck then added details and enthusiasm:

> Yesterday we went to Berkeley with a design for our traveling refrigeration plant and it is being built. Also ordered a Bausch and Lomb SKW microscope. This is a beauty with a side bar and drum nose piece. Primarily a dissecting microscope. My dream for some time in the

future is a research scope with an oil immersion lens, but that costs about 600 dollars and I'm not getting it right now. The SKW will be fine for the trip. But that research model, Oh boy! Oh boy! Sometime I'll have one. It may interest you that business at the lab is picking up. I can't tell you what this means to me, in happiness and energy. I was washed up and now I'm alive again, with work to be done and worth doing.[5]

In a letter a week later to his editor, Pat Covici, Steinbeck wrote,

Last night we had our Christmas with Carol's parents and tomorrow we set out north on a verification trip, the solstice tides being right for five days. So Xmas will find us in rubber boots and slickers, in the littoral north of San Francisco.

And the equipment of the truck goes on, beautiful equipment, a tiny pump, a small refrigeration plant, small aquaria, and a beautiful new microscope, bookcases and typing stands. All mounted in the truck. Very pretty. Insignia is $\pi\sqrt{-(R+S)^2}$. Don't think about this too much. It will drive you crazy. We don't want any publicity on any of this. It would be wrong.[6]

Recently, Ed Jr. discovered a notebook of his father's—labeled "Post Fire Notebook VII," assembled between September 28, 1939, and March 27, 1940—that sheds light on Ricketts's and Steinbeck's thinking at this time. In it Ricketts writes, "Because I will probably be interested in the factual history of this later on, at a time when I may be unable to reconstruct it, I will try now to delineate the rapid workings-out of this thing." He continues,

Jon *[sic]* has been saying that his time of pure fiction is over, that he'd like next to portray the tide pools, that his next work will be factual. He came down [to the Lab] this time depressed and unconfident, headed for a long walk or bus ride. He said that in February he and Crl [his wife, Carol] would go to Mexico. I said that if they'd wait until March I'd go along; that I wanted to go, that I'd rather go with someone who knew the ropes, and that I'd rather go with them. He said, "Fine," that maybe too we could get in a little collecting. I said that if I had any gumption I'd get busy first and get well started on the a/c [account] of SF Bay invertebrates that Stanf [Stanford] suggested I should do. Then Jon said, "Why don't we do that book together?" We talked it over a while and it began to seem to me quite feasible. So we began to lay plans for it, work to start immediately. Then somehow or other we got to talking about the Mexico trip; it changed around more and more from the idea of a motortrip down to Mexico City, to the idea of, primarily, a Gulf of California collecting trip. (Jon said, "If you have an objective, like collecting specimens, it puts so much more direction onto a trip, makes it more interesting.") Then he said, "We'll do a book about it that'll more than pay the expenses of the trip." And as we considered it, we got more and more enthusiastic about the whole thing.

We started at once to lay out plans, to write down lists of things to do, to get, to take, to plan our itinerary and activities . . . the idea of the book loomed up more and more as the significant feature of the whole thing. We both became quite sure that it could be a great thing, maybe very great, a modern Odyssey.[7]

Katie Rodger recounts that a few pages later, Ricketts wrote that they were suspending work on the Bay Area handbook and going to the Sea of Cortés.[8] Both men needed to get away. For Steinbeck, the backlash from *Grapes of Wrath* was intense, and his marriage to Carol was falling apart. Ricketts had recently ended an affair with a "married young woman"—some have said the love of his life—and he was deeply upset. In lieu of driving their truck down to Baja California they decided to charter one of the purse seiners from Monterey and go into the Gulf of California. Steinbeck agreed to bankroll the trip, and advanced expenses against the share of royalties Ricketts expected.

Four days before they set sail, Steinbeck hired the seventy-six-foot *Western Flyer,* owned and captained by Tony Berry. Ricketts wrote, "Our plans had to be violently changed still once more. The boat we had lined up had a change of heart at just the last minute, thought a few dollars more per day would be just lovely, especially since we were in such a hurry and therefore couldn't look around to get another . . . but we did get another, a far better boat. Charter all signed. Thank dee lawd for the Jugoslav fishermen."[9] The crew consisted of Tex Travis, engineer, and seamen Tiny Colletto and Sparky Enea. Carol Steinbeck also went, though her husband left any direct references to her out of his account.

Both John Steinbeck and Ricketts agreed to keep journals, but only Ricketts followed through. As Benson recounts, the collecting and processing of specimens was harder and more time-consuming than Steinbeck had thought it would be. He had considered writing notes and commentary along the way, not just for the purpose of the projected book but also for a series of articles he'd sell to help finance the trip. Two weeks into the trip he wrote, "We've been working hard collecting, preserving, and making notes. No log. There hasn't been time. It takes about eight hours to preserve and label the things taken at the tide. We have thousands of specimens. And it will probably be several years before they are all described."[10]

Ricketts's log from the trip and other notes he kept while aboard the *Western Flyer* were presumably lost until Ed Jr. recently unearthed "Post Fire Notebook VIII." According to Rodger, the last third of this notebook details plans for the trip, followed by the log and associated notes for the first seventeen days—from March 11 through March 27—of their six-week expedition.[11] Having not seen this log, Benson could write that the captain of the *Western Flyer,* Tony Berry, "had no use for Ricketts whatsoever— he didn't pull his weight and was soused most of the time. 'If Ricketts had had his way,' the captain judged, 'he would have gone down and anchored for six weeks and had a vacation.'"[12] The crew felt differently. While they didn't know what to make of Ricketts, they found him pleasant and liked him. Tex thought he was some kind of professor who had been fired from Stanford. So when Ed did some eccentric things, "like sit in a tub taking a bath for two or three hours at a time out on deck, Tex viewed them as activities that might be habitual for a type unfamiliar to him."[13]

The presence of this log, even though it covers only the first third of the trip, clearly indicates that Ricketts was doing more than Berry chose to see. This is natural. Berry's responsibilities were the boat itself, the safety of the crew, and getting the boat to where it needed to be when it needed to be there—low-note stuff. Ricketts's responsibility was to pull together all the reasons for doing the trip in the first place, including the scientific log, collecting notes, correct preservation and storage of specimens, and the eventual identification of the species collected (which, as one who has been on such expeditions, I can attest to its having been accomplished remarkably quickly—in months, not the years that

Steinbeck predicted)—high-note stuff. Low notes and high notes are not necessarily harmonious.

Ricketts's log from the trip includes notes from all aspects of their experience: scientific observations (sketches of the environment and of species collected, along with measurements), impressions of the people they met, and philosophical ramblings.[14]

The trip covered forty-one days and nearly four thousand miles of coastline.[15] According to Steinbeck's narrative portion of their joint publication, *Sea of Cortez,* the collection dates and locations were as follows:

March 17:	Cape San Lucas
March 18:	El Pulmo Reef
March 20:	Espíritu Santo Island
March 22:	La Paz/El Mogote
March 23:	San José Island/Cayo Islet
March 24:	Maricial Reef
March 25:	Puerto Escondido, outer
March 27:	Puerto Escondido, inner/Coronado Island
March 28:	Concepción Bay
March 30:	San Lucas Cove/San Carlos Bay
March 31:	San Francisquito Bay
April 1:	Angeles Bay
April 2:	Angel Custodio
April 3:	Red Bluff Point
April 4:	(listed erroneously as April 22 in *Sea of Cortez*) Puerto San Carlos
April 5:	Guaymas
April 8:	Estero de la Luna
April 11:	Agiabampo Estuary/San Gabriel Bay[16]

The *Western Flyer* docked back in Monterey on April 20. The task of sorting and identifying the more than five hundred species collected fell to Ricketts, and soon after unpacking he began sending unknown specimens to specialists. The Steinbecks left almost immediately for Mexico City to film the documentary *The Forgotten Village*. According to Richard Astro, Ricketts would have preferred that Steinbeck stick around to begin the narrative portion of the book, but as Rodger points out, "Steinbeck often needed time to process experiences before writing them, and his decision to take on another project was not out of character."[17]

Ricketts soon joined them. He drove the Steinbecks' car down to Mexico City and was supposed to assist in the film's production, but there was little to do. The rift that had developed following the collecting voyage apparently widened as Ricketts openly disagreed with Steinbeck about the premise of his film. Ricketts wrote to the Lovejoys, "I received a not very warm welcome—a possibility I had anticipated . . . I have seen almost nothing of Jon or Crl. I am off their list. . . . A new experience for me being the poor cousin. But being good natured and not holding grudges much makes it not so bad at all."[18] Ricketts noted in his journal, "There are things in which I excel: My sense of truth, my ability to understand a situation or a thing or a person or group. Of these things, my ability to go to the depths and fit them all into a unified field; to collect and collate information and to get the whole picture out of it."[19] While in Mexico City, he took advantage of the library at the Universidad Nacional Autónoma de México's Instituto de Biología to expand his literature base for the Sea of Cortés book.[20]

Eventually, the two men agreed to disagree and let the matter go.[21] Ricketts returned by train to Monterey and began to assemble the "Annotated Phyletic Catalogue and Bibliography," his formal contribution to *Sea of Cortez*. Steinbeck stayed in Mexico to finish his film, then returned to Monterey. After the first of the year finally began his narrative of the trip. On January 28, 1941, he wrote in his journal,

> I am down at P.G. [Pacific Grove] at Esther's [Steinbeck's sister's] house and just starting the gulf book. . . . Now the old laziness but I don't think it will hold me long. This is a comfortable house, with a rather good fireplace. I must not get into the difficulty of drinking as everyone down here does. This is the uphill fight with no end but clarity and no reward except the feeling that a decent job has been done. I wonder whether I can do it. . . . Hard things beginnings— very hard. But I must do them. And I can. It will be easy when once the start is made. And that start is going to be made, and that today. It should not be hard. I think I am going to enjoy just sitting here and writing. I'm pretty sure I am. It is comfortable and quiet. At night I can draw the curtains and it will be warm and nice. The inevitable thing happens. My busy little mind thinks up a hundred things I ought to do rather than the writing. I should think that at my age it wouldn't do that any more. Time is running out and at the end of this page I will go to the opening. And the opening should be good—very good.[22]

The next day, January 29, Steinbeck wrote, "And the opening was good, I think. Ed thinks so too. In fact, he thinks it is better than I do."

On May 19, Steinbeck wrote to his agent, Elizabeth Otis, "We got off a lot of [manuscript] to you which you probably have by now. It is more than Pat [Covici] asked for. A brutally peremptory letter from him to Ed this morning demanded it."[23]

In 1947, Steinbeck wrote to his friend Bo Beskow, "When I wrote the text of the Sea of Cortez, Gwen [Conger, Steinbeck's lover at the time and a few years later his second wife] and I were hiding in the pine woods in a cabin and she would sleep late and I would get up and build a big fire and work until noon when she woke up and that would be the end of work for the day and we would go walking in the sand dunes and eat thousands of doughnuts and coffee." Steinbeck added, tongue fully in cheek, "I worked very hard."[24]

Ricketts and Steinbeck built the book throughout 1941, and it came together rapidly. Ricketts's common-law wife (he was still legally married to his first wife, Nan), Eleanor "Toni" Jackson,[25] began typing the catalog and bibliography sections; later, Steinbeck hired her to type his narrative.[26] In the book Ricketts acknowledges Jackson, "who, in addition to manuscript revising and glossary constructing, transcribed the bulk of the difficult text, both journal and appendix, the latter phase involving that most vexing of all secretarial tasks—the editing of scientific copy interlarded with handwriting of doubtful legibility."[27] The illustrations were done by Alberté Spratt; color photographs were contributed by Russell Cummings and others, including W. K. Fisher, who had previously skewered *Between Pacific Tides*.

On July 4, 1941, Steinbeck wrote to Covici, "'still shaky' from having finished a first draft of 'Sea of Cortez.'" Later, in the same letter, he wrote, "See if the manuscript sounds like drinking." And finally, "This book is very carefully planned and designed Pat, but I don't think its plan will be immediately apparent. . . . I even think that it is a new kind of writing. I told you once that I found a great poetry in scientific thinking. Perhaps I haven't done it but I've tried and it's there to de done."[28]

Two weeks later, on July 18, Steinbeck wrote to Otis, "We are working like beavers and should finish second draft about next Wednesday, that is of my part. Pat says he wants carefully corrected second draft rather than waiting three weeks for perfect third draft so we will send it to you as soon as it is corrected. I think it reads pretty well."[29]

On August 22, 1941, Ricketts wrote to Steinbeck,

> It seems gratifying to reflect on the fact that we, unsupported and unaided, seem to have taken more species, in greater number, and better preserved, than expeditions more pretentious and endowed, as we were not, with prestige, personnel, equipment and financial backing. As Toni says: "Two guys in a small boat, with enthusiasm and knowledge."
>
> It appears that our unpretentious trip may have achieved results comparable to those of far more elaborate expeditions, and certainly more unified and ordered in an architectural sense. It may well prove to be, considering its limitations, one of the most important expeditions of these times.[30]

Sea of Cortez was published by Viking on December 5, 1941, but the events at Pearl Harbor two days later and the subsequent entry of the United States into World War II overshadowed the book's release. While Steinbeck wrote to Toby Street, "The reviews of The Sea of Cortez are extremely good and lively," the book got little attention and sales were low.[31] Ricketts wrote, "Royalties on the book have so far been nil, and again I am afraid I fathered a financial flop."[32]

Intercalary III

For many people with an environmental perspective, *A Sand County Almanac* is a must, their favorite book of all time. For many others, it is *Sea of Cortez*. What is astonishing about these breakthrough works is that their brilliance was not initially recognized. Early sales were not good. *Sand County* sold steadily but not spectacularly; profits were sufficient to keep the book in print until society had been primed to accept it. Steinbeck's name alone may have kept *Sea of Cortez* afloat. Then, after Ricketts died, the narrative was reissued as *The Log from the Sea of Cortez,* with a new section titled "About Ed Ricketts." Steinbeck was listed as sole author. It is this edition that began to gain traction.

Because of the competitive world we inhabit, it is tempting to compare *Sand County* and *Sea of Cortez* with an eye to determining which is "better." This would be a mistake. While both works have their origins in natural history (indeed, in shacks) and messages that are timeless, they are separate books holding different meanings. With *Sand County,* Leopold wanted to instill in society an ethic—a voluntary form of individual restraint to curb a purely material focus—when addressing issues pertaining to the natural world. In *Sea of Cortez,* Ricketts and Steinbeck sought something in the lives of humans akin to the unified field theory in physics. They wished to combine science and religion into a larger, more inclusive philosophical structure that could serve as a guide to living a life that is rich and full, and packed with meaning. These are not competing concepts; Leopold showed us what to do, Ricketts showed us how to do it. So as compelling as these books are by themselves, together they send a message to the world that is more powerful than either considered alone, one that transcends the discipline of ecology and extends into every nook and cranny of society.

Today, for many people, living a meaningful life requires a conscious effort to embrace the natural world—think of the concept of "nature deficit disorder" and initiatives to combat it such as "no child left inside." The trick is to convert what is now a matter of individual perspective into a broad societal consensus, and to promote a general realization that the future of humanity may depend on such a shift in consciousness. The perspectives of Leopold and Ricketts are so far removed from the way that society in general now operates that examining their underpinnings becomes both interesting and instructive.

CHAPTER TEN

Daily Lives and Professional Expectations

If Aldo Leopold and Ed Ricketts had ever shared the same shack (in fact, they never met and were probably unaware of each other's existence),[1] there would have been every chance that at any particular point in the day, someone would have been awake. Neither slept much. Besides that, Leopold was a morning person to the extreme, awakening at 3:00 or 4:00 A.M. At the Shack he would make a pot of coffee, go outside, get out his notebook, and record birdsongs. In Madison, he'd walk to his office and put in a few hours before anybody else showed up. He'd go home for lunch and a nap, and then return. His evenings were short; he was frequently in bed by 9:00, even when hosting guests. Ricketts—as befits one who lived across the street from a brothel—was a night owl. Friends would come over in the afternoon or evening, and gatherings would often carry on until dawn.

Although he rarely demonstrated it as an adult, Leopold remained an individualist his entire life. As with many with a touch of genius, he was "solitary in his ways," and "chafed under social conventions."[2] Meine writes, "He was in many respects an enlightenment personality confronting the realities of the twentieth-century world, with the benefits of twentieth-century ecological science at hand."[3] True to this nature, Leopold was a bottom-up thinker, an inductive thinker; to him, everything started with observation, and generalizations were built from there. He was a keen observer, and the words that Bob de Roos had for Ricketts, "the best eyes I have ever seen at work," also hold for Leopold (and, in fact, for every first-rate biologist I have ever been around). But it was his well-honed ability to draw inferences (and occasionally broad implications) from his observations that formed the basis of Leopold's legacy.

Leopold's powerful intellect was belied by a quiet, patient, reciprocal approach to his relationships with family, colleagues, and students. Unlike so many accomplished professionals working today, he was secure and confident in his abilities, so much so that he did not need to show them off, or keep reminding others of the talents he possessed. In part, these qualities were what drew students to him, and made them intensely loyal once they were aboard.

At first blush, Ed Ricketts's most distinctive features were his hands and eyes. According to J. J. Benson, he had the hands of a surgeon or artist—long fingers, with a gentle but firm touch that matched his personality.[4] He was accepting, almost completely without malice, yet had a kind of sure, inner toughness.[5] He had enormous charm, not phony or superficial, usually accepted foibles, and didn't reject people because of them. The mature Ed Ricketts was a remarkable and complex man, and largely because of Steinbeck he has become a legend, making it very difficult to distinguish the qualities of the man from those of the legend. Joel

Hedgpeth points out that Steinbeck's portrait of Ricketts as Doc in *Cannery Row* "is the only full treatment of a marine biologist in English fiction. In the popular imagination, Ricketts has become Doc, a loveable character who lived just as he wanted to live, getting enough to drink, eat, listen to and go to bed with, and in the end, to read. In the minds of some students, all this is what you do when you are a marine biologist and the learning comes just as easy as the wine, women and song."[6]

Also clouding the reality of Ed Ricketts were the almost unanimously favorable reactions of those who knew him, reactions that sometimes approach idolatry.[7] He was a hardworking, highly rational biologist who sought and uncovered scientific truths, yet he was also eccentric. He lived freely and had little concern for societal constraints. At some level Leopold would have appreciated him. In a statement that sounds like paradox, Leopold once wrote, "Nonconformity is the highest evolutionary attainment of social animals."[8]

Part of what made Ricketts so unusual was the fact that the humanities—art, music, literature, and philosophy—were as much a part of his life as the natural sciences. As Benson points out, Ricketts's basic approach to life and to understanding it was one of synthesis; his approach to biology was often as much philosophical as it was scientific.[9] Ricketts was open and honest—probably too open for his own good. Benson writes, "People simply could not cope with that honesty, and it added considerably to the pain of his very complex relationships with women."[10] As Vonnegut once observed, "the truth can be really powerful stuff. You're not expecting it."[11]

Also complicating Ricketts's life was his vision of individual freedom. Benson notes that Ricketts felt "people should be free to act as they truly felt and that they should not be restrained either by convention or by the demands or expectations of others. He felt that . . . two people should come together in freedom, without demands, obligations, or forms, to establish such mutual bonds as each might desire for as long as both might consent."[12] This approach to life emerged from Ricketts's personality. Hedgpeth observes that Ed Ricketts was a man "full of love with such an extraordinary and gentle humor, and such a gift for friendship."[13] He never tired of looking at animals on the shore, and he was especially delighted to see children learning things. Carol Steinbeck remembered that his eyes would take on an almost phosphorescent glow during such interactions.[14] During a trip to the Outer Shores, Ricketts once told a missionary priest, Father Mulvihill, whom he greatly respected, that his idea of heaven was to be out on the reef "at low tide when the sun was rising and the marine life was just teeming."[15]

There were differences between Leopold and Ricketts in their daily lives and professional expectations. During the final two decades of his life Leopold was a university professor, salaried and tenured, with graduate students and an undergraduate teaching load that included courses in his field of wildlife ecology. Ricketts was a serious, haggard small businessman. He gathered, processed, packaged, and sold biological specimens to high schools, colleges, and universities. Most of these specimens he collected himself. His catalog offered mainly marine creatures, from microscopic organisms on slides to rays, octopuses, hagfish, starfish, jellyfish. He also dealt in such laboratory staples as rats, cats, and frogs. Ricketts was honest and tried to be a good businessman. He kept good records, but because he worked alone, or with amateur help, he would sometimes get behind, and the business would get muddled.[16]

There were other professional differences. Leopold was paid to think (and boy, did the University of Wisconsin get its money's worth). Ricketts was not (though this did not stop him). The way Ricketts spent his time determined his near-term salary, and time spent pondering stole from time spent generating income. As he wrote to his daughter, Nancy Jane, "As for bringing home the bacon I was never too hot."[17] Each man clearly created for himself a lifestyle that suited his personality, although toward the end of their lives this idyll was compromised. Leopold had health issues, first with his eyes, then with sciatica, and later with sporadic, severe facial pain (tic douloureux, also known as trigeminal neuralgia). For Ricketts, the combination of broad interests, weariness from running the Lab business for twenty years, and the effect of World War II on the domestic economy choked Pacific Biological, and therefore his financial flexibility.

The lasting image of Aldo Leopold is of him sitting on a bench outside the Shack, alone at daybreak, sipping coffee and writing field notes, with birdsong and rustling leaves in the background, the air smelling organic and fresh from the nearby river.

The lasting image of Ed Ricketts is of him sitting cross-legged on his bed in his Lab, sipping beer late at night, with friends gathered, working through the material that formed his worldview, the surf lapping in the background, the air smelling light and salty.

And with these images in mind, it is time to ask, What were these men thinking?

CHAPTER ELEVEN

From Natural History
to Ecology

Much of what both Leopold and Ricketts pondered was the emerging discipline of ecology, and what ecology was beginning to tell us about humanity's proper place in the world. They were considering their society's emphasis on putting people above nature or outside of nature, and the derivative of this view, the human domination of nature—what people today call shallow ecology, wherein value is seen as residing in human beings, and nature is given merely use value or instrumental value.[1] Leopold and Ricketts contrasted this view with the one that they were developing, wherein human beings are viewed as an intrinsic part of nature, a mere panel in a large quilt—what people today call deep ecology. It was from this perspective that Ricketts convinced Steinbeck that ecology was both an important and a much-neglected truth, a new way for people to understand their relationship with nature—the most powerful idea of the twentieth century and "perhaps the key to the future."[2]

To put their era into context, we turn to a historian of natural history, Robert Kohler. According to Kohler, the history of field biology reflects three stages:

1. the geographically extensive and serendipitous collecting characterizing the early age of exploration and empire (from the late fifteenth century to about 1880), when studying nature was viewed as pious;

2. the extensive and intensive methods of the middle age of survey (from the 1880s to the 1930s); and

3. the local and highly intensive collecting that exemplifies the current age of ecology (from the 1930s to the present).[3]

Kohler's first age—exploration and empire—was driven by personalities. Key naturalists during this time comprised a handful of men whose names remain familiar, including John Ray, Mark Catesby, Erasmus Darwin, William Bartram, Jean-Baptiste Lamarck, Alexander von Humboldt, John James Audubon, Louis Agassiz, Charles Darwin, Alfred Russel Wallace, and Asa Gray.

Kohler's second age—survey—was dominated not so much by personalities as by the human processes of settlement and cultural transition; this was especially true in North America. According to Kohler, between the 1880s and the 1930s the natural environments of North America were in transition, readily accessible by rail and increasingly by road, yet still relatively wild.[4] And with this accessibility, attitudes about nature were changing, as wilderness became less threatening. Outdoor recreation—including camping, mountain walking, mountain climbing, hunting and fishing, rural cottaging, and amateur naturalizing—encouraged an interest in nature.[5] The Boy Scouts and Girl Scouts were formed about this time, as were YMCA camps.

In addition, Kohler notes, a new fashion for second, vacation homes emerged, a trend that included, for the first time, middle-class families.[6] And this fad led (interestingly, given our focus on Leopold's Shack) into a rage for buying abandoned farms. "The idea of owning an 'abandoned farm' captivated [the] imagination, and a mini-landrush ensued."

With this interest in the outdoors came an enthusiasm for the animals and plants living there. Kohler notes that sporting magazines such as *Chicago Field* (later *Field and Stream*) and *Forest and Stream* were filled with natural history pieces by distinguished American naturalists, especially ornithologists, ichthyologists, and mammalogists.[7] At that time, the high reputation of *Forest and Stream* made it a legitimate means of communication among naturalists. Prominent ornithologists such as Elliot Coues and Robert Ridgway contributed, as did David Starr Jordan, America's premier ichthyologist.

From the 1880s into the 1930s, museums and government surveys dispatched large numbers of expeditions per year to collect specimens and map the distribution of species. Museums involved included large civic institutions, such as the American Museum of Natural History in New York, the Field Museum in Chicago, and the Academy of Natural Sciences in Philadelphia.[8] Research museums at several universities, including Harvard's Museum of Comparative Zoology, the Museum of Vertebrate Zoology in Berkeley, California, and the University of Michigan Museum at Ann Arbor, also dispatched expeditions. The U.S. Biological Survey, lead by C. Hart Merriam, was sending out up to a dozen field parties a year, primarily to the American West. Natural history surveys (including the still-extant Illinois Natural History Survey) were operating. Field stations were established. And by the 1920s, other organizations such as newspapers and magazines,

the National Geographic Society, and commercial biological supply companies were sponsoring expeditions (which puts Ricketts's
Lab into the context of its day).[9] By the early 1890s, more than one
hundred commercial firms dealing in natural history specimens
and collecting paraphernalia advertised in the pages of Samuel
Cassino's *Naturalists' Directory.*

Kohler describes these surveys as organized and systematic, an
exacting science. And unlike the previous era's individual collectors, explorers, and naturalists, who gathered and recorded "whatever serendipity offered up" without a plan, museum and state
surveys collected systematically and thoroughly, with the goal "to
create collections that were not just samples of a region's fauna
or flora but were comprehensive and complete embodiments of
its biodiversity."[10] By applying uniform collecting practices and
meticulous data management, surveys were designed to make the
study of natural history exact and rigorous.

These collections then provided baseline data for producing
species classifications and biogeographic maps. Biogeography
addresses questions such as where creatures live, and why they
live there. And once these data are known, they contribute to
our growing understanding of biodiversity. According to Kohler,
"The history of our knowledge of biodiversity is first and fore-
most a history of collecting and collections."[11] Today, our knowledge of biodiversity is anchored by these early surveys. It is these
data that allow us, through subtraction, to document the number
of species going extinct as a result of human pressures, generating
concern that in our ecological ignorance we are destroying the
workings of ecosystems upon which our own survival may hinge.

Whereas Kohler's second age—survey—gave us the biological
parts to work with, his third age—ecology—gives us the means to

understand how these parts fit together. One marker of this transition is the formation of the Ecological Society of America in 1915. While ecology can be defined in many ways, perhaps the easiest way to visualize organismal-environmental interactions is as a hierarchy ranging from the individual level to the global level. Individuals form populations, populations of different species interact to form communities, communities interact with abiotic (nonliving) factors such as geography and climate to form ecosystems, ecosystems combine to form ecoregions, and ecoregions combine to form global (biospheric) patterns.

The history of ecology roughly parallels this hierarchy. Early ecologists focused on the morphology of organisms as explained by environment. For example, Bergmann's rule, formulated in 1847, asserts that within a species, body mass increases with increasing latitude or altitude (colder climates), while Allen's rule, formulated in 1877, states that animal appendages (limbs, tails, ears, noses) decrease in length in colder climates.[12] By the first half of the twentieth century, ecology had moved toward focusing on interactions within populations and the factors that influence the assemblage of populations into communities. In his 1931 book *Animal Aggregations,* Ricketts's mentor, W. C. Allee, noted that the birthrate per capita declines at low population densities (now known as the Allee effect), and in 1935 Cabrera stated his law of ecological incompatibility, defined in chapter 5.

Leopold and Ricketts were born during the first half of Kohler's age of survey, and as they matured professionally, they were influenced by, and helped to drive, the transition to the age of ecology. This in itself is unusual, for as Howard Gardner points out, "Most individual scholars are born and die within a single paradigm."[13] Fittingly, Kohler uses Leopold's good friend Herb Stoddard as one example of a professional who made this transition.[14] Stoddard, talented but without an advanced degree (or for that matter even a high school diploma), was a naturalist and junior taxidermist at the Milwaukee Museum when he was chosen for a job as a research biologist for the U.S. Biological Survey. He went on to a distinguished career in the ecological discipline Leopold founded, wildlife biology, and became the world's premier expert on bobwhite quail and their management.[15]

Leopold spoke like a twentieth-century ecologist, using terms such as *biotic pyramid, food chain, energy circuits, species diversity,* and *home range;* however, he referred to himself by a nineteenth-century term—as a naturalist:

> History has not conspired to make my task an easy one.
> We naturalists have much to live down. There was a time
> when ladies and gentlemen wandered afield not so much
> to learn how the world is put together as to gather subject
> matter for tea-time conversation. This was the era of dickey-
> bird ornithology, of botany expressed in bad verse, of ejacu-
> latory vapors such as "ain't nature grand." But if you will
> scan the amateur ornithological or botanical journals you
> will see that a new attitude is abroad. But this is hardly the
> result of our present system of formal education.[16]

Meine points out that Leopold used the term *ecology* judiciously, and sometimes had difficulty communicating its meaning to students, except in the field, where he could keep one foot in traditional natural history and the other in modern science. "His aim was to teach others how to take a given field situation, recognize and weigh the variables on display, and connect those variables in time and space."[17]

Leopold's secretary, Vivian Horn, recalled, "I learned the word 'ecology' at this time. It was not a common word in those days. Even if I did not fully comprehend the significance of what I was typing, many others did not fully comprehend it either, judging by the belated recognition of his work."[18]

In 1939, Joseph Grinnell wrote to Leopold, "some of our potent professors do not grant the worthiness, or even the existence, of a 'field ecology.' You have probably heard of such in your neck of the woods! The combination of forestry, botany, and zoology looks to them like ecology, even though I myself [take] pains to avoid the word!"[19]

Leopold realized that he was in this transitional period, and wrote in *A Sand County Almanac,* "Ecology is an infant just learning to talk, and, like other infants, is engrossed with its own coinage of big words. Its working days lie in the future. Ecology is destined to become the lore of Round River, a belated attempt to convert our collective knowledge of biotic materials into a collective wisdom of biotic navigation."[20]

One sign that Ed Ricketts was also making the conversion from collection/survey thinking to ecological thinking was the difficulty he had in publishing *Between Pacific Tides.* This was a book based on the old natural history tradition of collection, but couched within the new framework of ecology. For example, when Ricketts and Joseph Campbell went to the Outer Shores in 1932, Campbell wrote,

> We had collected for weeks in an environment free from ground swell and surf. Then suddenly, within a few miles, both appeared, we were again on open coast. And more than coincidentally, the whole nature of the animal communities changed radically, more than it had in a thousand miles of inner waterways. The species were different, their

proportions were different, they even occurred differently. The fauna of the surf swept rocks outside Sitka resembles that of the similarly exposed California coast nearly 2000 miles distant more than it does that of similar type bottom protected from surf only three miles away . . . some powerful environmental factor must sort out the sheep from the goats.[21]

Reviewers didn't know how to handle a book with one foot in the old paradigm and one in the new. They were unknowingly, or perhaps stubbornly, behind the times. Even Ricketts's old adviser, W.C. Allee, was marking this transition. Allee's first book, *Animal Aggregations,* published in 1931, focused on a mid-level emphasis in ecology—interactions among species—while his second book, *Principles of Animal Ecology,* published in 1949, showcases an early mature view of this new discipline.

Overlaid upon this transition in natural history from curio collecting to the serious scientific discipline of ecology was the Dust Bowl—the defining event that made ecology suddenly relevant. As Timothy Egan explains, prior to the Dust Bowl, in the early 1920s, the Federal Bureau of Soils proclaimed, "The soil is the one indestructible, immutable asset that the nation possesses. . . . It is the one resource that cannot be exhausted, that cannot be used up."[22] But then homesteaders, encouraged by government settlement programs, plowed up the Great Plains for wheat farming, and in the process extirpated the vast communities of prairie plants. These native plants, drought tolerant and with root systems extending dozens of feet into the subsoil, had held the soil in place for millennia, in a way that wheat could not, and eventually would not.

Drought combined with high-plains winds lifted the bare dirt.

Dust storms took the form of huge rollers, and their color provided a clue to origin: black dust came from Kansas, red from eastern Oklahoma, yellow-orange from Texas.[23] In Pampa, Texas, Woody Guthrie watched as a roller approached, figured what was about to happen, and wrote, "So long, it's been good to know ya."[24] Some storms were enormous; one on May 9, 1934, held three tons of topsoil for every American alive.[25] The dust was abrasive, and with strong winds scraped the paint off houses.[26] People stopped shaking hands in greeting because the static electricity was so great it would knock them down.[27] Journalist Ernie Pyle drove across the Great Plains and wrote of "this withering land of misery . . . the saddest land I've ever seen."[28] When people along the eastern seaboard and in Washington, D.C., began to see dusty skies and taste fresh topsoil from the plains, two thousand miles away, they finally believed the stories they'd been reading and realized for the first time that out West something had gone wrong with the land.[29]

They also realized that it was something caused by man, a by-product of hubris and ignorance on a grand scale.[30] An inch of topsoil can blow away in an hour, but it takes a thousand years to restore it.[31] As Egan points out, "one man cannot stop the soil from blowing, but one can start it."[32] And not only was it a case of man affecting land, it was a case of land affecting man. The 1930s was the first decade in U.S. history in which the number of young children declined.[33] The question was, If humans caused it, could they fix it? Maybe. But to do so, they would have to rethink how they approached the land. Enter Aldo Leopold.

CHAPTER TWELVE

Leopold's Approach

Nina Leopold Bradley wrote in her remembrance, "A Daughter's Reflections," "In an essay found among my father's works, he had written, 'there are two things that interest me: the relation of people to each other, and the relation of people to land.'"[1] More than anything else, it is this second interest that forms the basis of what we think about when his name is mentioned. And it is this curiosity that drove Leopold's ecological thinking.

Franklin Roosevelt's adviser on soil, Hugh Hammond Bennett, wrote, "of all the countries in the world, we Americans have been the greatest destroyers of land of any race of people barbaric or civilized." The Dust Bowl, he said, was "sinister," a symptom of our "stupendous ignorance."[2] But, as Timothy Egan notes, "Most scientists did not take Bennett seriously. . . . Basic soil science was one thing but talking about a fragile web of life and slapping the face of nature—this kind of early ecology had yet to find a wide audience. Sure, Teddy Roosevelt and John Muir had made conservation an American value at the dawn of the new century, but it was usually applied to brawny, scenic wonders: mountains, rivers, megaflora." Egan then points out that "in 1933, a game biologist in Wisconsin, Aldo Leopold, had published an essay that said man was part of the big organic whole and should treat his place with special care. But that essay, 'The Conservation Ethic,' had yet to influence public policy."[3]

In the 1920s and through much of the early 1930s, when Leopold used the term *land* he usually meant "soil." His interest in soil quality and stability came from his early days as a forester in Arizona and New Mexico, where he saw firsthand the effects of grazing on stream courses and the surrounding landscape. This interest continued with, indeed was reaffirmed by, the drought of the middle 1930s and the Dust Bowl that followed. But later, Meine explains, as new experiences and his seminal work at the Shack influenced his thinking, "Leopold was using the word 'land' as a catch-all term for the environment; it included 'soils, water systems, and wild and tame plants and animals.'"[4]

In 1936 and again in 1937, Leopold traveled to Chihuahua, Mexico. Here, he said, he "first clearly realized that land is an organism, that all my life I had seen only sick land, whereas here was a biota still in perfect aboriginal health. The term 'unspoiled wilderness' took on a new meaning."[5] Appreciating this, he became increasingly interested in defining what he called "land health." He turned to science, and recognized that "stability and diversity were the [ecological] concepts that seemed best suited for a critical appraisal of land, be it a wilderness or a dust bowl." He then asked, "What, in the evolutionary history of this flowering earth, is more closely associated with stability? The answer, to my mind, is clear: diversity of fauna and flora."[6] Although this insight seemed intuitive to Leopold, and seems intuitive to us, as a general rule the relation between diversity and stability is not well grounded in fact; ecologists have struggled, and continue to struggle, with defining broad relationships between these two ecosystem concepts.[7]

Much to his credit, Leopold realized that he was reaching "beyond the range of scientific evidence." In the late 1930s, most ecologists had not even reached the point of asking questions about ecosystem qualities, let alone gathered data to measure them. Leopold wrote, "The best we can do, at least at present, is to recognize and cultivate the general conditions which seem to be conducive to [stability]. Stability and diversity are associated. Both are the end-result of evolution to date. To what extent are they interdependent? Can we retain stability in used land without retaining diversity also?"[8]

Leopold expanded this thinking to consider land as an organism, and he wasn't simply thinking metaphorically. "The land consists of soil, water, plants, and animals, but health is more than a sufficiency of these components. It is a state of vigorous self-renewal in each of them, and in all collectively. Such collective functioning of interdependent parts for the maintenance of the whole is characteristic of an organism. In this sense the land is an organism, and conservation deals with its functional integrity, or health." Summarizing, Leopold wrote, "Conservation is a state of health in the land."[9]

In his early reflections, Leopold also began exploring the factors that destabilize ecological relationships (i.e., that produce poor land health). High on his list was technology. He wrote, "Rural education has been preoccupied with the transplantation of machinery and city culture to the rural community, latterly in the face of economic conditions so adverse as to evict the occupants of submarginal soils."[10] Leopold continued, "Technology raises the land's carrying capacity for man; it increases man's 'take,' but it has so far ignored the 'give,' and further ignored the adjustments man forces onto other animals and plants. It has also assumed that man's 'take' from the land, as well as human population, can be increased indefinitely." Leopold then applied the lessons of ecology to humans, "Technological innovation might very well continue to increase food supplies, but ecology teaches that food is not the only, or even the main, limitation on animal populations. Usually, some other limitation kicks in before food supplies are exhausted."[11]

Leopold drove home his main point: "Each technology has its own yardsticks, usually yields or profits. But only commercial land uses have any profit, and some of the most important land uses have only spiritual or aesthetic yields. The collective criterion must be something deeper and more important than either profit or yield." In choosing an example, he turned to the land. "Among the ordinary yardsticks, I can think of but one which is obviously a common denominator of success in all technologies: soil fertility. That the maintenance of at least the original fertility is essential is now a truism, and needs no further discussion."[12]

And then Leopold neatly tied up his argument, "There can be no doubt that a society rooted in the soil is more stable than one rooted in pavements." And he told us where the root of the problem could be found. "Stability seems to vary inversely to the mental distance from fields and woods. The disruptive movements which now threaten the continuity of human culture are not born on the land where the take originates, but in the factories and offices where it is processed and distributed, and in the capitols where the rules of division are written."[13]

Leopold was exploring all aspects of his arguments, and one of them, as the previous sentence suggests, was the role of government. Leopold briefly considered a method of achieving land health through government intervention, which he then rejected. As Meine writes, "Leopold had a Jeffersonian faith in democracy: the only sure cure for democracy's ills was still more democracy. Simply put, if citizens wished to avoid the undue imposition of government, then they had to assume responsibility for conservation on an individual basis." Leopold's perspective originated from a blending of practical needs and his own personal brand of conservatism—the solution did not lie in government programs. "Government actions, necessary though they were, no matter how good they were, could not stem the tide of land abuse. 'One of the curious evidences that "conservation programs" are losing their grip,' Leopold wrote, 'is that they have seldom resorted to self-government as a cure for land abuse.'" He continued, "We who are about to die, unless democracy can mend its land-use, have not tried democracy as a possible answer to our problem." As Meine writes, from Leopold's perspective, "trying democracy" meant learning how to tell good land-use from bad, using one's own land accordingly, and refusing aid and comfort to those who do not. Leopold felt this brand of democracy was more relevant than "merely voting, petitioning, and writing checks for bigger and better bureaus, in order that our responsibilities may be laid in bigger and better laps."[14]

Having dismissed government intervention, Leopold next turned to the people themselves. "The basic defect is this: we have not asked the citizen to assume any real responsibility. We have told him that if he will vote right, obey the law, join some organizations, and practice what conservation is profitable on his own land, that everything will be lovely; the government will do the rest." The problem was, "This formula is too easy to accomplish anything worthwhile. It calls for no effort or sacrifice; no change in our philosophy of values. It entails little that any decent and intelligent person would not have done." And in one of the most important sentences Leopold ever wrote, he generalizes the conservation problem to all problems: "No important change in human conduct is ever accomplished without an internal change in our intellectual emphases, our loyalties, our affections, and our convictions." And he continues, "In our attempt to make conservation easy, we have dodged its spiritual implications. The proof of this error lies in the fact that philosophy, ethics, and religion have not yet heard of it."[15] As Meine points out, Leopold felt that conservation lacked a sense of personal responsibility in our relationship with land—an "ecological conscience." Meine continues, "Leopold's philosophy had come to a sharp point. Still squeezed between a stubborn reluctance to hand responsibility over to government and the reality of public indifference to that responsibility, he chose the only other alternative: a forthright assertion of individual responsibility for land health."[16]

Leopold knew he was entering new territory when he wrote in his article, "The Ecological Conscience," "The practice of conservation must spring from a conviction of what is ethically and esthetically *[sic]* right as well as what is economically expedient. A thing is right only when it tends to preserve the integrity, stability, and beauty of the community, and the community includes the soil, waters, fauna, and flora, as well as people."[17] Others knew, too. As Meine notes, a number of periodicals had published "The Ecological Conscience," and Leopold's reprints were soon gone. He received many letters, including one from Max Otto, on the faculty at the University of Wisconsin's Department of Philosophy. Otto wrote, "I like the combination of frankness and restraint which you achieve. These are praiseworthy qualities I see in things, and to come upon them always gives me new confidence." Then he got to his main point. "Still, I value even more a quality in your paper which I can only call *spiritual*. You have a *philosophy of wildlife management* which is itself part of a philosophy of life." And in closing he offered a hope, "I wish religious people—*church* people, I mean—could see it to be part of religion to enlist your cause. I'm afraid most of them do not see life in these terms."[18]

Leopold had moved beyond his ecological training and vast scientific experience into a philosophy—a new worldview. He asked what developments could bring stability to the landscape, and then answered: the formulation of mechanisms for protecting the public interest in private land, and the revival of land aesthetics in rural culture. He wrote that out of these forces a land ethic might eventually emerge, "but the breeding of ethics is as yet beyond our powers. All science can do is safeguard the environment in which ethical mutations might take place."[19]

Meine notes that this was the first time that the phrase *land ethic* appeared in any of Leopold's writings or lectures. And while the term Land Ethic eventually became synonymous with Leopold's philosophy—indeed, with the man himself—Leopold rarely used the term, and then only toward the end of his life. The problem wasn't with the words, but rather with Leopold's own aversion to moralizing. Meine writes, "Leopold was not a preacher. He despised demagoguery, and chafed under social conventions. Ethics were a personal matter, weighed by the individual, not dictated by authority. An individualist to the core, he was confronting the complex reality of twentieth-century environmental problems, with the quality of life, for both people and the land, held in the balance." And Meine points out that at this point in his life, Leopold was not prepared to go beyond "Land Pathology" in defining his Land Ethic. But in light of the Dust Bowl, he began to rethink the foundations he had laid in "The Conservation Ethic."[20]

When Leopold was finally ready to define his Land Ethic, it went like this: "A thing is right when it tends to preserve the integrity, stability, and beauty of the biotic community. It is wrong when it tends otherwise."[21] And this early ecologist, with his bottom-up style of thinking, moved beyond his science to a philosophy, an ethic—a voluntary form of restraint—that he felt humans must adopt if society (and perhaps our species) were to persist. This, in Leopold's view, reflected humanity's proper relation to nature. As Michael Lewis has written about people such as Leopold, "Civilization made them men of learning, but in order to save it they must leave their studies and become men of action."[22]

Ed Ricketts occasionally looked in the same direction. Eric Tamm writes, "In the tide pools of the outer shores, with war in the Pacific nearing a cataclysmic end, Ricketts became intent on searching for not just a greater understanding of animal life, but also an ecological basis for human ethics. He grew convinced that his discoveries in the tide pools could help restore the balance in a shattered world."[23]

CHAPTER THIRTEEN

Ricketts's Approach

While Leopold's worldview was ecological and utilitarian (what J. B. Callicott has called a transformative vision), Ed Ricketts's worldview was ecological and holistic (what Callicott calls a transcendent vision).[1] According to Richard Astro, Ricketts used the principles of ecology to grasp and understand the totality of things. His search for order was centered on a quest to find "our emotional relationship to the world conceived as a whole, . . . 'a unified field hypothesis' in which 'everything is an index of everything else.'"[2] While most biologists, including Leopold, tended (and still tend) to view ecology as individuals having relationships, Ricketts viewed ecology as relationships having individuals. That is, for Ricketts, the relationships were often primary; who or what was having them was secondary. It was this emphasis, extended in an internally consistent way to his own behavior, that created many of Ricketts's personal problems. Unlike Leopold, Ricketts was not particularly interested in voluntary forms of restraint.

There were other differences between the ways that Leopold

and Ricketts thought. On the one hand, Leopold defined ecology in utilitarian terms, with imposed value judgments—"Ecology tries to understand the interactions between living things and their environment. Every living thing represents an equation of give and take. Man or mouse, oak or orchid, we take a livelihood from our land and our fellows, and give in return an endless succession of acts and thoughts, each of which changes us, our fellows, our land, and its capacity to yield us a further living. Ultimately we give ourselves."[3] On the other, Ricketts defined ecology in holistic terms of acceptance, as "the study of relationships, of living relationships." He wrote, "I got to thinking about the ecological method, the value of building, of trying to build, whole pictures. No one can controvert it. An ecologist has to consider the parts each in its place and as related to rather than as subsidiary to the whole."[4]

One of Ricketts's best explanations of his worldview came in 1940. His friend, modernist composer John Cage, was teaching concepts of music in the Bay Area. In December Ricketts and Cage returned to Monterey together. In a letter to Toni Jackson about the trip, Ricketts wrote,

> [John Cage] and I had a very pleasant trip back. We worked out an understanding, almost a statement of our differences of viewpoint. It involves, as I suspected, a real honest to god fundamental, a right or left turn up the steep mountain, and surely involves in culture that same primitive cleavage apparent now in government: as an individual or a communal point of departure. And he represents the probably upcoming thing. Divine inspired geometry is a good term. A square or a black line is more nearly the same for all people—therefore a great leveller—than a folksong or a picture of a cow or a Shakespeare sonnet, or more even

than the tones or words etc. of which they're composed.
But all my tendencies are toward 'meaning,' while his are
toward 'organization' as such. I regard content as primary,
he form. It's more than the old controversy, it represents
actually a fundamental divergence (although I still think
it's the mountain that's of deepest importance). And his is
unquestionably the purest thing.[5]

As Astro points out, Ricketts used ecology as he consciously
worked toward a method by which man might recognize and
understand the relatedness of living things.[6] Ultimately, Ricketts settled on a philosophy that he called "breaking through."
He took the label from Robinson Jeffers's poem "Roan Stallion"
("Humanity is the mould to break away from, the crust to break
through"), and defined breaking through as an "inner coherency
of feeling and thought which leads man into a 'deep participa-
tion' and enables him to tie together apparently unrelated pictures
and see that 'the whole is more than the sum of its parts.'" Further, he wanted to "achieve that integrative moment of living in
which one understands things 'which are not transient by means
of things that are.'"[7]

Astro notes that Ricketts tried long and hard to find a means
by which he could communicate "the deep thing."[8] The method
Ricketts chose he inappropriately called nonteleological or *is* thinking. This view is laid out in the March 24, Easter Sunday, chapter (chapter 14) of *Sea of Cortez,* which was taken nearly verbatim
from his essay on nonteleological thinking. Ricketts's explanation
of the concept of "*is* thinking" suffers from an awkward use of
philosophical terminology, which Ricketts himself admitted. By
insisting that teleological thinking is associated only with the eval-
uation of causes and effects and their relative purposefulness, with

an end pattern of what "could be" or "should be," Ricketts carves off a portion of the concept of teleological thinking from its "total philosophical and etymological context."[9]

What Ricketts is really talking about is an open, ecological approach to life by the person who looks at events and accepts them as such without judgment, reservation, or qualification. In doing so, people perceive the whole picture by becoming an identifiable part of that picture. Ricketts suggests that the nonteleological method of thinking is capable of "great tenderness, of an all embracingness," which comes with the love and understanding of instant acceptance: "*what* they are is unimportant alongside the fact that they *are*. In other words, the 'badness' or 'goodness,' the teleology of the fears [is] decidedly secondary." Ricketts continues, "this non-causal or non-blaming viewpoint seems to me to [arise] emergently from the union of two opposing viewpoints, such which comprises infinity in factors in symbols might be called mystic."[10] As Katie Rodger points out, "Nonteleological thinking was likely an amalgamation of Ricketts' interests in [Carl] Jung, mythology, ecology, and philosophy. . . . Ultimately, Ricketts believes, nonteleological thinking enables an individual to live more fully: as questioning decreases, acceptance increases, and a person moves closer to holistic awareness, or transcendence."[11]

In addition to his essay on nonteleological thinking, Ricketts wrote essays on "The Spiritual Morphology of Poetry" and "The Philosophy of 'Breaking Through,'" which, he stated to Joseph Campbell, "pretty much sum up the world outlook, or rather inlook, that I have found developing in myself more and more during the years."[12] But Ricketts didn't just stop once he had constructed his philosophical framework. As with Leopold and his concept of land, Ricketts played with his philosophy the way a cat worries at a mouse. Rodger writes, "[Ricketts] constantly revised and refined his ideas based on discourse with his talented friends through letters and discussion, attempting to better articulate his thoughts."[13] Ultimately, Steinbeck best summed up Ricketts's approach to life in his novelette, *Cannery Row*. As Benson writes about the themes of *Cannery Row*, "What is life, what is death, and what do they mean? [Steinbeck] also asks what are the most important things in life? The answers are simple: life is a process; death is part of life; neither life nor death mean anything—they simply are; and the most important things in life are love and beauty, which bring joy to the process of living."[14]

We know that Ricketts understood Leopold's approach to ecology when Ricketts wrote, "I got to thinking about the ecological method, the value of building, of trying to build, whole pictures. No one can controvert it."[15] We also know that in Ricketts's attempt to tie everything into everything through his process of "breaking through" he incorporated the concept of intuition (one mechanism of breaking through), which Leopold certainly used (the essays in *Sand County Almanac* are full of intuitive perceptions) but didn't formally acknowledge.

Ricketts's view of intuition derived from Jung's, of "a perception by way of the unconscious" that is "possibly the most proximate way to transcendent function."[16] Ricketts called himself an intuitive thinker and noted that such people have "atypical emergent functions" in that they are "concerned with the inner world of spiritual (to them) realities." He described this as "an instant of connection—or integration—between an individual and the universe, a flash of breaking through, or transcendence. . . . It's all part of one pattern. . . . I suspect now that the pattern is universal, that we fail to see the transcending simplicity of it only because of obstacles on our inward horizons." This challenge of breaking through the "obstacles on our inward horizons" (through intuition in many cases) to achieve some higher level of awareness was the philosophical cornerstone of Ricketts's worldview.[17]

It is interesting that many things Ricketts termed spiritual or mystical have explanations centered in science, explanations that were at least hazily available to the scientists of his time. The mystical line "everything is an index of everything else" has scientific merit in the sense that life on earth was likely created only once, and that, if this is true, all living things are descended through common ancestry—we are all (admittedly distant) branches from the original form of life.[18] If we generalize to include both living and nonliving entities on Earth, Ricketts's phrase still makes sense because the molecules we have available to us now are the molecules that have always been present on Earth (plus asteroids, meteors, comet dust, and other space stuff that survived atmospheric burn and crashed to the earth's surface; minus the manmade space hardware that has escaped earth's gravitational pull). If we generalize "all things are one" to include all that is the universe, we are still on pretty solid scientific ground, because everything that exists is thought to have been created by the Big Bang and derives from it.

Similarly, Ricketts's notion of insight through intuition is beginning to be understood by neuroscientists. There is a region in the nondominant lobe of the brain (typically the right hemisphere—roughly 95 percent of humans are left-hemisphere dominant), in an area called the superior frontal gyrus of the cerebral cortex, where scientists think intuitions are formed.[19] That is, the ability to intuit, just like other forms of intellectual (and athletic, as it turns out) activities, is not only hard-wired, but also can probably be improved upon with proper training. Despite appearing to be a mystical attribute to the early twentieth century mind, intuition, we now know, is—as with all mental functions—an organic property.

While Ricketts's approach to science (and his adoption of the new science of ecology) is best exemplified by *Between Pacific Tides,* and his overarching philosophy by *Sea of Cortez,* his mature, holistic, ecological viewpoint is most visible in his attempts to understand the collapse of the West Coast sardine fishery (which took with it the economy of Cannery Row). Ricketts recognized the role that overfishing, especially of young animals and of adults during spawning aggregations, played in reducing commercial sardine stocks. But he was also one of the few scientists who recognized the role that climate and food (plankton) availability played in sardine abundance, and how these ecological factors could be temporally variable within regions, and spatially variable across regions.[20] As Rafe Sagarin and Larry Crowder have recently pointed out, Ricketts's approach to the sardine fishery reflected a modern, holistic, ecological approach that is called ecosystem-based management, an approach that extends beyond single species management to consider species interactions and habitats within a framework that includes the viewpoints of multiple stakeholders. Sagarin and Crowder further point out that ecosystem-based management has been criticized because commentators emphasize what, from their point of view, should be instead of agreeing on what is, and that adoption of Ricketts's non-teleological approach would improve this situation.[21] As with Leopold, Ricketts's ecological ideas remain relevant today; not only were they ahead of his time, but in some ways they also remain ahead of ours.

CHAPTER FOURTEEN

Shared and Complementary Perspectives

As noted above, throughout his life Leopold tended to be a loner, "not social, not antisocial." His closest friends were found among his professional colleagues, graduate students, and family. He was a solitary thinker who returned to an early interest in wild game management after a long convalescence, and who later in life relied heavily on the personal observations and data gleaned from his Shack experiences. Leopold seemed to work on his ideas alone, waiting until they were formulated and composed to pass manuscripts around for comment. Most of Leopold's major works did not involve direct collaboration. He was immersed in his discipline, and this interest was extended to his children, all of whom maintained a professional-level interest in science. Starker, a wildlife conservationist, who died in 1983, and Luna, a geomorphologist, who died in 2006, were held in such regard that they were elected to the National Academy of Sciences. Estella is a paleobotanist who has also been elected to the National Academy of Sciences. Carl is a plant physiologist who founded and directs the influential nonprofit Tropical Forestry Initiative, centered on rain forest reforestation projects in Costa Rica. After an early career as an ecologist, Nina now lives near the Shack and has been active in initiating and sustaining, in all sorts of ways, the Aldo Leopold Foundation.

Ricketts, on the other hand, was social. His closest friends were not biologists—in fact, there were few biologists on the West Coast in the early twentieth century and those who were present not only did not share Ricketts's interests, but seemed to have feelings about his occupation that ranged from aversion to hostility. Instead, he associated with writers, artists, and other sorts of bons vivants and freethinkers. His Lab facilitated social gatherings, which in turn aided his thinking. Both of Ricketts's books were composed in collaboration with professional writers. His son, Ed Jr., understood the underpinnings of his father's way of life and chose for himself a lifestyle that gave him immense personal freedom.[1]

It is curious that although Leopold and Ricketts were superb field biologists and took similar, highly detailed notes (in fact, both recorded field notes in sometimes illegible print; Leopold's notebooks were black and letter-size, Ricketts's were usually green and legal-size), their views of science could not have been more different. Ricketts viewed science as a process, a way of knowing, proceeding "from observation to speculation and ultimately to hypothesis (and this, says Steinbeck, 'is the creative process, probably the highest and most satisfactory we know')."[2] Leopold, on the other hand, chose to personify science. He wrote, "Time was when the aim of science was to understand the world, and to learn how man may live in harmony with it. If I read Darwin right, he was more concerned with understanding than power. But science, as now decanted for public consumption, is mainly a race for power. Science has no respect for the land as a community of organisms, no concept of man as a fellow passenger in the odyssey of evolution."[3]

As Meine observes, "Leopold questioned the 'soundness of the assumptions on which the whole modern [societal] structure is built. If science cannot lead us to wisdom as well as power, it is surely no science at all.'"[4] However, Leopold could see both sides of most issues, and he wrote, "Modern science has saddled us with many vicious ideas; so many that it seems to me to have become a doubtful honor to be called a scientist. But science has also made one contribution to culture which seems to me permanent and good: the critical approach to questions of fact."[5] But as Meine points out, "Leopold's criticism of science in general did not prevent him from encouraging advancements in his own field. Under his guidance . . . younger researchers were working new lines of study in wildlife behavior, physiology, endocrinology, nutrition, population ecology, refuge management, and endangered species. The scope of the science had broadened immensely."[6]

Neither Leopold nor Ricketts trusted the growing scientific trend toward specialization. Leopold disregarded, even disrespected, interdisciplinary boundaries. And in *Sea of Cortez,* Steinbeck and Ricketts wrote, "A few naturalists had gone into the Gulf and, in the way of specialists, had seen nothing they hadn't wanted to."[7] Further, as Astro indicates, "Ricketts was horrified at the growing tendency toward scientific specialization; he believed that so-called experts who carefully localize their interests so that they can boast that they know *one* thing well really have no organon at all."[8] According to Ricketts, specialists are "vegetables planted too long in one soil which secrete toxins and inhibit their own prosperity." Ricketts also believed that any kind of "intensive specialization, vegetable or intellectual, is self-defeating in that it destroys the dynamic unity in nature."[9] The discipline of ecology, as understood by both men, could not be neatly categorized into more traditional academic fields.[10]

When viewing Leopold's and Ricketts's contributions to the early science of ecology and an approach to living based on a fundamental knowledge of natural history, it is clear that there were shared emphases. As Eric Engles has pointed out, both men understood that we must rely on science, done right, to show the way. Both men knew that to gain understanding one must observe and study nature directly, openly, and deeply.[11] Ricketts wrote, "The whole picture should be stressed, and one's feet should be kept firmly on the ground by frequent actual collecting, by observing how the animals live and by constant open-minded checking."[12] Reflecting this feet-on-the-ground emphasis, Leopold called his approach a Land Ethic. Both men knew that ecology is based on relationships (although Leopold took the traditional approach that organisms have relationships, while Ricketts took the unconventional viewpoint that relationships have organisms). Both men had grave suspicions about an emphasis on reductionism at the expense of holistic understanding (in fact, reductionism has become a much-lamented reality throughout modern science, as we shall see below).

There were also unique contributions and emphases by both men, based on their distinct interests and personalities. Leopold, anchored by his science of wildlife ecology, sought to achieve a method for balancing human needs with those of other organisms. His strategy was to establish an ethic based on minimizing the negative impacts of humans on the natural world. Ricketts, with his talented friends and broad interests spanning science, art, and literature, emphasized the whole picture. While Leopold derived an ethic that he hoped would be adopted by all members of society, Ricketts derived a philosophy to be used as a guide for living his own life.

Though not dogmatic, Leopold was often unapologetically judgmental. His Land Ethic incorporates beliefs about good and bad land use, and he sought to influence policy. Ricketts resisted this temptation to judge; he was less interested in influencing the behavior of others. As Eric Engles has pointed out, at a personal level, Ricketts was likely just as concerned about ethical behavior toward nature as was Leopold, but this is very different from going out of his way (as Leopold did) to try to persuade society to develop an environmental consciousness. Ricketts may have been sad that people didn't respect nature, but he did not seem to expect people to decide consciously to adopt ethical behaviors toward the natural world.

One way to emphasize this difference in approaches is to record what each of them had to say about being affected by a smile. In September 1924, Leopold went to the Mayo Clinic in Rochester, Minnesota, to have minor surgery on his jaw. There were delays and complications with the procedure, and during his waiting time he walked around town observing the Minnesotans. He saw a "short and pink and very shaven" businessman whom he dubbed "little Elk," who wore, as Leopold put it, "the most beautific [sic] smile." And he followed this up: "The smile haunted me. I admired it, and rather felt gratified that this system of ours should provide so limited a person with sufficient thrills to engender it."[13] In contrast, when Ed Ricketts was on his 1945 Outer Shores trip, he wrote, "I was walking along the float and I saw one of those things that moves me so much. A young Indian woman, sickish—maybe tb, the rate is said to be high here among the natives—and with an [abscessed] eye, carrying a baby." He quickly generalized, "It was the old business of people in trouble and taking it and being wonderful, 'something that happened.'" And then he did a typical Ed thing, "I smiled at the woman and really meant it and she smiled back in that wonderful way that Indians do." And again the generalization, "I haven't ever seen such illumination in a white; it just gives you that marvelous sense of contact that transcends language and custom."[14]

We note these differences and know there is some degree of truth in each perspective, yet Leopold and Ricketts were complicated men who often resisted generalizations. There were times when Leopold was (at least tacitly) accepting, while Ricketts was occasionally more judgmental. For example, regarding Leopold's approach to religion, Meine writes, "Aldo remained absolutely mum on the subject of religion. . . . The children could sense, however, that he took a dim view of it. The spiritual aspect did not bother him; it was the sober discipline and oppressive orthodoxy, so foreign to his own upbringing, that he could not abide." But children are smart and Leopold did not have to speak directly to them about religion. Through his careful attention to the natural world, especially at the Shack, and his "career-long efforts to address human dilemmas through conservation, Leopold managed to accomplish through the back door what he had vowed to not broach through the front. The children were gaining an awareness of life's processes, of creation itself, that was unencumbered by middlemen."[15]

Ricketts also was not religious, and for much of his life did not approach the subject of religion as openly as he regarded other aspects of his life. He viewed the Catholic Church "skeptically" and disagreed with its narrow-mindedness and "slightly ridiculous framework."[16] At one point he fought an ultraconservative priest on the teaching of sex education and liberal arts at the local high school in Monterey.[17] More generally, Ricketts distrusted organized religion and thought it "deadish or cultish or wishful."[18] But then, on September 11, 1946, Joseph Campbell and his wife, Jean, visited Ricketts. Campbell sold Ricketts on his notion that religion could be "pragmatically valuable;" that "churches, with their insistence on value beyond the temporal and material, could sublimate or at least temper the thirsty individualism of the free market by 'insisting on a regard for suprapersonal values.'" Following this discussion, Ricketts wrote, "A good many religious ideas may not hold water intellectually and scientifically, but they certainly do socially."[19]

There can be no doubt that Leopold and Ricketts lived and breathed ecology, even when contemplating circumstances that were far from ecological. They both had sons stationed in the Pacific during World War II (Ricketts himself was drafted into the army and served in Monterey). Carl Leopold was a Marine, a first lieutenant, and because secrecy was necessary for security, he was forbidden to give his location. At one point, the Leopolds had not heard from Carl for a month and did not know his whereabouts. When his letter finally arrived, Carl kept the tone upbeat as he described the local birdlife, which enabled Aldo to determine where he was stationed.[20] Carl recently wrote,

> My first assignment in the Pacific was in the defense of
> the Palmyra, a small atoll in the Christmas Island group.
> This was a relatively quiet place, and there were myriads
> of interesting birds there, Japanese love-birds (nesting),
> boobies, frigate birds, and many sandpipers. The atoll is

now a nature preserve. Anyhow, I had a chance to watch the birds on the atoll, as we were well equipped with binoculars. I was surprised when a cluster of curlews appeared. I would guess that it might have been in April 1943. In a letter home, I mentioned this unusual sighting, innocent of any knowledge about the migration of curlews.

Dad knew that Arctic curlews made the huge flight from the Antarctic to the Arctic with only a stop in the Christmas Islands. So Dad cleverly and correctly inferred that I was there. Certainly I was not intending to reveal where I was. I was reporting only interesting bird species that I had seen.[21]

In February 1945 Carl came home on leave, and Aldo and Estella met him and his wife, Keena, at the train station in Madison. As Meine writes, "Carl had never before seen his father weep."[22]

Ed Ricketts Jr. was drafted into the army in March 1943, and, as with Carl Leopold, was sent to the Pacific Theater, where he worked on MacArthur's staff. In August Ricketts wrote to his son, offering advice typical for a marine biologist: "See and record everything you can; you have to be seeing for me too, because probably now I'll never get anywhere off the Pacific Coast of NA. At one time I thot I might have a look at Hawaii, or the Grt. Barrier Reef of Australia, but now I know my life will be already too short for me to finish up the Pac. Coast of NA invertebrates."[23]

On January 5, 1944, Ricketts wrote to Ed Jr. of hearing "that you were incommunicado, taking shots, and probably destined for the close-up fighting front. I suppose that's part of the pattern, and something that most of the younger generation wouldn't willingly miss, but this older generation don't like the idea so well."[24] And after the war Leopold, the ecologist, wrote in an unpublished essay, "we are now confronted by the fact, known at least to a few, that wars are no longer won; the concept of top dog is now a myth; all wars are lost by all who wage them; the only difference between participants is the degree and kind of losses they sustain."[25]

Ricketts also had a general distaste for the war and the waste of resources. In 1945 he wrote that if warring countries "could only junk their defense (and offense!) military budgets, devote that money and thought and energy to the common enemy— degenerative diseases, public health, psychiatry and human relations including especially international relations, problems of the distribution of goods, what a difference that would make in our human misery and our bad dreams and our unexplained personal depressions." Then he made his argument personal: "To believe [our sons], sensitive people all, could devote their life energy to interesting and constructive things rather than to getting along with a bunch of men in the army."[26]

Leopold and Ricketts were spectacular men. But neither, by himself, completed the vision of ethic and engagement demanded by the current environmental movement. This is not surprising. They were early workers in a new field at a time when communication was primitive and travel took effort. Both have been faulted for having shortcomings when viewed from the perspective of our time. This is mistaken. Instead, they should be embraced for being so impressively progressive as judged by the standards of their time, and in some cases still by the standards of ours.

Intercalary IV

Leopold and Ricketts were born into the age of natural history and as mature scientists helped to form the emerging discipline of ecology. In retrospect, we can see that the power of Leopold's and Ricketts's ecology derived from its foundation in the practices and preoccupations of natural history. But today, ecology has moved on, and much of it is no longer grounded in natural history. As Eric Engles has noted, since the late 1940s, ecology has drifted towards specialization, abstraction, theoretical modeling, and even reductionism, and this has been to its detriment as a discipline that can influence public policy and therefore society at large.[1] Steven Herman has been more direct: "My guess is that Aldo Leopold regularly rolls over in his modest grave at some of the circumstances and practices of modern wildlifery. . . . I think the thing he would most lament is the decline of the role of natural history in the study and practice of wildlife biology." Herman elaborates, as follows: "I find considerable evidence that wildlife management has broken partially free of its roots and is showing signs of malnourishment." Among its problems include "addiction to technology, lust for statistics, professional hubris, and the delusion that research and management are synonymous." And he offers some history. "The wildlife management discipline [whose patron saint was Aldo Leopold] started as applied natural history, and most of its star practitioners were broad-based naturalists, intimate with the landscapes and organisms in their charge. There are reasons to believe that the wildlife profession would do well to re-graft itself to those natural history roots."[2]

As Herman points out, the *history* in natural history refers to the old use of this term, and means "description." He also notes that as the discipline of ecology arose, the "use of the terms 'natural history' and 'naturalist' fell into disuse and even disrespect." Herman defines natural history as "the scientific study of plants and animals in their natural environments. It is concerned with levels of organization from the individual organism to the ecosystem, and stresses identification, life history, distribution, abundance, and inter-relationships. It often and appropriately includes an esthetic [sic] component."[3] I suspect that both Leopold and Ricketts would have wholeheartedly agreed.

Paul Dayton extends this reasoning, and again, I expect Leopold and Ricketts would have agreed: "Natural history is the foundation of ecology and evolution science. There is no ecology, no understanding of the function of ecosystems and communities, no restoration, or in fact, little useful environmental science without an understanding of the basic relationships between species and their environment, which is to be discovered in natural history."[4]

Today it is worth asking, If the spirit of Leopold and Ricketts does not lie in our tendencies toward specialization, which permeate not only wildlife biology, but also the larger field of ecology, science in general, and society as a whole, is it gone?

CHAPTER FIFTEEN

Transcendence

On Thursday, April 22, 1948, Dan Thompson, one of Leopold's students, and his research assistant were driving south along U.S. Highway 51 in northern Wisconsin when the news of Leopold's death came over their car radio. Stunned, and perhaps thinking about nothing so much as an emptier and more questionable future, they drove a long way in silence.[1]

In the spring of 1948, Ed Ricketts had been making plans for another Outer Shores trip. In Clayoquot Sound on Vancouver Island, Bill and Ruth White had just received a letter from him on Pacific Biological Laboratories stationery. It was newsy and announced that he would be up in just over a week. As they read, their radio was playing, and the news of Ricketts's death was announced. Shock must have met perplexity: how could Ed be both dead and alive?[2]

Three days after Leopold's death, Bob McCabe, Joe Hickey, Leopold's secretary, and his typist drove from Madison down to Burlington, Iowa, and the Aspen Grove Cemetery, where Leopold was buried in the Starker family plot. In his grief, McCabe played the role of critic: "The pastor who conducted the brief ceremony could have used some of A.L.'s skill to say properly what might have been a tribute in farewell." And once he returned to Madison, McCabe wrote, "A long period of readjustment had begun."[3]

Ed Ricketts's funeral was held in a chapel above the ocean, and a crowd, including the Lab group, gathered outside. When the chapel was opened, some of the mourners entered and saw the gray coffin draped with an un-Ed-like purple artificial wreath. After a moment they turned to leave and started walking, following a path down the hill. Some of the crowd continued into the chapel, but others instead turned away, following those leaving. They straggled down the hill to the seashore. One by one they found a place on a rock or in the sand to sit. In sad silence they watched, without really seeing, the water ebbing and flowing in the tide pools.[4]

When Leopold died, at least half of the sixteen thousand pines he and his family had planted, along with a prairie restoration, had taken hold.[5] The Leopold children had grown and, except for Estella Jr., had dispersed, and the Shack had few visitors. After Leopold died, farmers in the area turned their properties—a total of twelve hundred acres—into a management trust called the Leopold Memorial Reserve.[6] Today, its cornerstone is the new, beautifully conceived, energy-efficient Leopold Legacy Center. Built from pines that Leopold had planted (harvested to maintain healthy tree densities), the Legacy Center serves as a multipurpose facility designed for both research and education. When the Legacy Center was being built, the organizers put out a call for volunteers, and more than three hundred people showed up—a testament not only to the power of Leopold's ideas, even today, but to the community of extraordinary people who call the Baraboo Hills region home.[7]

Ricketts's Lab had a different fate. Bruce Ariss writes that after Ricketts died, "Steinbeck went back to New York, but since he owned the note on the Lab, he soon after sold the place to Jack [Yock] Yee, a Cannery Row landlord, who was the owner of the Wing Chong grocery store building across the street."[8] The Lab sat empty for three years. In May 1951, Harlan Watkins and Ed Larsh—an artist who was part of the Lab club after Ricketts's death—were driving down Cannery Row. As Larsh tells the story, Watkins, an English teacher at the [Monterey Union] high school, was looking for a place to stay, and wondered if he could rent Ed Ricketts's Lab. He went into the Wing Chong grocery in search of Yock Yee. The three of them crossed Cannery Row and climbed the Lab stairs. According to Larsh, the Lab "was as if Ed Ricketts had left the day before—a little musty, some personal belongings scattered about. His record player, silent now, still held a Gregorian Chant. There were many other old records, mostly classical. In his collection we found two jazz albums; one a single record of Duke Ellington's greatest hits with his big 1940s band featuring Harry Carney on bass sax and Johnny Hodges on alto, the other, a record of the famous Benny Goodman rendition of 'Sing-Sing-Sing.'" Yock Yee and Harlan struck a rental deal for forty dollars a month.[9]

Much later (July 1994), Ed Jr. returned to the Lab. He told Larsh, "I lived at the Lab from 1937 'till I was drafted in late 1942. Then I returned to the Lab in 1945 and stayed with my dad until his death in 1948, when he was killed at the rail crossing up on Drake Street. I was around until John Steinbeck sold the Lab to

Yock Yee. Then one afternoon after packing my bag, and taking one last look around, I closed the door and walked down the
stairs."[10]

Bruce Ariss comments on, and then ends the story about Harlan Watkins's rental of the Lab. "As an English teacher at the
high school . . . I think it gave him quite a bit of prestige with his
creative writing classes." Later, when Watkins was about to get
married and move out of the Lab, he had an idea: "Why not form
a men's club and buy the old building to preserve it from destruc-
tion, and then maintain it as sort of a literary monument?"[11] And
that's what happened. About twenty artists and professional men
chipped in and purchased the Lab for an affordable price. This
group eventually included cartoonists Hank Ketcham (the creator of the cartoon strip *Dennis the Menace*), Eldon Dedini (whose
work was featured in *Esquire, The New Yorker,* and *Playboy*), and
Gus Arriola (the creator of the comic strip *Gordo*). According to
Larsh, when Ed Jr. walked down the Lab stairs for the last time
as a young man, he left about six hundred jazz records, which
Ritchie Lovejoy saved.[12] Fittingly, among the group who bought
the Lab were men who would eventually birth the Monterey Jazz
Festival, and its first organizational meetings were held in the Lab
(Ricketts would have loved this). In the early 1990s, this group of
now-older men, aware of the history of the aged building and not
wanting it destroyed, sold the Lab to the City of Monterey, which
restored the structure and occasionally opens it to the public.

Leopold's memory lives on at the University of Wisconsin,
where his former students, Bob McCabe and Joe Hickey, replaced
him. It lives on through his talented children and students, and
through the continuously growing number of fisheries and wildlife biologists. It lives on at the Shack, where family and friends

continue to gather and to work, and at the Legacy Center. It also lives on in *A Sand County Almanac,* which sold steadily, if modestly, until the mid-1960s. Then, following the publication of Rachel Carson's *Silent Spring,* the environmental movement took hold and *A Sand County Almanac* became one of its bibles. By now it has sold more than a million copies and inspired biographies and books of essays and criticism about Leopold. It spawned this book.

As Joel Hedgpeth has noted about Ricketts, "Ed's best talents were his wit, his capacity to see the humor of situations and his ability to converse and participate with people. . . . These are ephemeral graces."[13] Ricketts's memory lives on in the minds of his friends and his children. It lives on in Steinbeck's work, including *Cannery Row* and its nostalgic sequel, *Sweet Thursday.* Steinbeck mentions Ricketts in *Travels with Charley;* probably a day never went by without him thinking of Ricketts. Ricketts's memory lives on through *Between Pacific Tides,* which remains in print, and in Steinbeck's reissued *Log from the Sea of Cortez,* especially in the added section, "About Ed Ricketts." It lives on in Cannery Row, where the Lab still stands and continues to host some of Monterey's best thinkers (and drinkers). From 1979 to 2003, the Moss Landing Marine Laboratory employed the research vessel (RV) *Ed Ricketts.*[14] The Monterey Bay Aquarium Research Institute currently employs the RV *Western Flyer* (named after the sardine boat Ricketts and Steinbeck took into the Sea of Cortés) and the brand-new submersible remotely operated vehicle (ROV) *Doc Ricketts.*[15] Ricketts's memory also lives on through his admirers. In 2004 a group of scientists, led by Bill Gilly of the Hopkins Marine Station, and writers rented the seventy-three-foot wooden trawler *Gus D* and retraced Ricketts and Steinbeck's Sea of Cortés trip.[16] Thanks to Katie Rodger and Eric Enno Tamm, Ricketts's groupies are now called "Ed Heads."

Today Leopold and Ricketts have thousands, perhaps tens of thousands, of admirers. There are clear differences between these two fan bases. Leopold's followers seem part of a group. They have not only a place to go—the Shack, a quiet place that lends itself to wonder and contemplation—but also, with the Leopold Legacy Center now completed, a place to gather. They have shared activities: planting trees and converting cropland back to prairie. My friends the Mossmans (Mike was one of the first Leopold Fellows), the Bakers (Dick studied with Estella Jr.), the Sorges, and the Caspers have participated in these projects, and so have hundreds of other families; the landscape of the Upper Midwest is different and richer because of them.[17]

Ed Heads are not so much a group as a collection of individuals. Discovering Ricketts seems to be a solitary thing, and as Geoffrey Dunn has noted, "Everyone who encounters Ricketts wants to claim him for their own."[18] Ricketts's fans have a place to go—the Lab. But unlike the Shack, huddled in a quiet woods along the bank of the Wisconsin River, the setting of the Lab on busy, touristy Cannery Row does not at this time in any way promote the Lab, lend itself to quiet contemplation, or facilitate gatherings. Ed Heads go there, stand across the noisy street, and look, or climb the Lab stairs and touch. They know what they're seeing, and in a sea of sightseers, know they are alone. They hold a secret, an intimacy, a knowledge that in this place and at this time, among all the humanity before them, only they truly understand. This sense is similar to, and may be the origin of, their proprietary feelings for Ricketts.

CHAPTER SIXTEEN

Ethic and Engagement

Leopold formalized the mature view of his Land Ethic sixty years ago, and as a philosophy it garnered wide appreciation forty years ago. But appreciation is not acceptance. The impression is that all we need to do is empower individuals with the right philosophy and the right information and they will follow, en masse.[1] This certainly hasn't happened. If the ecological ideas underlying the Land Ethic are true, and if they are right, and if they represent the most powerful idea of the twentieth century and the future of humanity depends on them, why haven't these ideas been embraced by mainstream society?

Convincing humanity to adopt the idea of an economy couched within an ecosystem framework might be the biggest challenge of the twenty-first century. Economist Herman Daly has distinguished between quantitative expansion (growth—the current economic model) and qualitative improvement (development—based on sustainability), and between "empty-world" economics (in which inputs and outputs are unconstrained) and "full-world" economics (in which constraints, including finite resources, are included as inputs and by-products, such as habitat loss and pollution, are included as outputs). He argues that a sustainable economy should be based on the concepts of qualitative improvement and full-world economics. Daly also knows the resistance his ideas face and notes, "There are enormous forces of denial aligned against this necessary shift in vision and analytic effort, and to overcome these forces requires a deep philosophical clarification, even religious renewal."[2]

Why this deep reluctance to shift our approach toward how we do business? According to Jung, just as our bodies retain vestiges of obsolete functions in many of our organs, so our minds echo the dim bygone in thought processes, including thoughts that view nature as something to be conquered.[3] Following Jung, and retracing a line of thought pursued by Ricketts and Joseph Campbell, the "mind features" that served humankind for most of human existence, when people were few and scattered and fighting for evolutionary survival, are not the mind features that will work today to guarantee the future of our species. Stephen Jay Gould knew this, and quipped that our real evolutionary legacy lies in the deep fallacies of current reasoning.[4] These vestiges create the current human paradox, and especially the paradox of humans living within the construct of "the American way of life." The future of humanity lies not in the old mind-set of individual self-preservation, but rather in the new comprehension that all life, even human life, must fit within the limits of Earth's ecosystems.

It's a tough sell. Ricketts and Steinbeck perceived that in today's world the features that we universally admire, such as wisdom, tolerance, kindliness, generosity, and humility, are "invariable concomitants" of failure, while features such as cruelty, greed, self-interest, and rapacity are regarded as the cornerstones of success.[5] As Michael Pollan observes, "Evolution may reward interdependence, but our thinking selves continue to prize self-reliance. The wolf is somehow more impressive to us than the dog."[6]

While one of the Jungian features of the human mind certainly is a focus on staying alive, Steinbeck perceived the irony in such obsession. He noted, "Preoccupation with survival has set the stage for extinction."[7] He named the enemies of mankind's future as "comfort, plenty, security"—the very attainments that early man, and early Americans, sought, but that in excess have been converted to a "poverty of spirit: cynicism, boredom, and smugness." As Steinbeck lamented in a 1959 letter to Adlai Stevenson, "we can stand anything God and nature throw at us save only plenty."[8]

Once people become preoccupied with personal gain, they easily lose track of the big picture. It's a scale issue, something that Ricketts and Steinbeck clearly knew and recognized early on: behaviors that may be good at the level of the individual, such as self-interest, may or may not be good at the level of the species. Vonnegut writes, "The biggest truth to face now—what is probably making me unfunny now for the remainder of my life— is that [we are so self-absorbed] I don't think that people give a damn whether the planet goes on or not . . . I know of very few people who are dreaming of a world for their grandchildren."[9]

In our preoccupation with the old issue of our own survival, humans—especially modern Americans—don't usually bother to think ecologically, within the confines of broader, sustainable systems. And even when we do, we are challenged by the differences between ideas and actions. As Steinbeck and Ricketts observe, "conscious thought seems to have little influence on the direction of our species."[10] Michael Lewis writes more bluntly, "When I started writing I thought if I proved X was a stupid thing to do that people would stop doing X . . . I was wrong."[11]

We need to find a way out. We need to couple the "rugged individualism" of not only a Jungian past, but also a pioneering American tradition—so often used in modern times to argue for the status quo—with the flexibility of behavior necessary to respond in creative ways to social and environmental change. As Leopold wrote, "No important change in human conduct is ever accomplished without an internal change in our intellectual emphases, our loyalties, our affections, and our convictions."[12] One way to overcome people's resistance to changing their views and behaviors involves a synthesis of Leopold and Ricketts's worldviews.

In *A Sand County Almanac* Leopold addresses how one can lead an *ethical* life (well grounded in the land, and in biodiversity), while in *Sea of Cortez* Ricketts addresses how one can lead an *engaged* life (with broad interests that span conventional topics and approaches). Both approaches—a melding of each man's ideas—may be required for change. As Leopold wrote in his essay "Natural History: The Forgotten Science," "Do people mend their ways out of calamity? I doubt it. They are more likely to do it out of pure curiosity and interest."[13] Pure curiosity and interest were the centerpieces of Ricketts's worldview. So while Leopold shows us what to do, Ricketts shows us how to do it. Together these ideas create a unified, natural history–based worldview representing something broader than ecological thinking. The benefits of a more natural history–focused ecology (and a more ecologically focused biology) extend far beyond the practice of science. As Eric Engles has pointed out, such an approach to understanding the natural world, and our own unnatural world, is far easier to "sell" to the public, more intrinsically interesting when taught in public schools and in universities, and builds upon a better foundation for informing ecologically responsible citizens (the basis of Daly's economic lament).[14] In short, the way out might just be found in the spirit of both Leopold (ethic) and Ricketts (engagement); in truths derived from natural history, created in old buildings looking out on and observing the modern world.

CHAPTER SEVENTEEN

Where Their Spirit Lives On

The spirit of Leopold and Ricketts persists, and there is some welcome evidence that it may be growing. It lies, at its most basic, in shacks, buildings that provide access to nature but do not get in the way. It is there in the hundreds of "rubber boot" biologists, usually working alone and often with little fanfare at remote sites—often field stations. It is found after midnight, in the mist over a springtime wetland, with spring peepers calling close by and crawfish frogs in the distance. It is found in a couple of beers and a cool, late-night skinny dip after a long, hot day on a short-grass prairie. It is found among the smells inside old stone lab buildings. It is there in the eureka moment—an observation, and the realization that in the entire history of Earth and its humans, this is the first seeing.

The spirit of Leopold and Ricketts is found in the rhythms of curators working in the back rooms of public museums; in the smells of their alcohol and formaldehyde, and the flip side smell of emerging into fresh air. It resides in the research and rearing facilities of zoos and aquariums, where for some species, the last of their kind exist. It is found in the field trip—a professor driving and chatty, the van full of eager students. This spirit is deep in the graduate student who, with ruler and notebook in hand and soaked to the skin in the middle of a driving spring squall, says, "I'd still rather be doing this than sitting in front of my laptop."

The spirit of Leopold and Ricketts is found in the ideas that question convention and move a discipline forward, not in the ideologies that constrain and dictate.[1] It is found in the many biologists who left the federal government over the past eight years because they would not be compromised, and in the many other biologists who stayed in order to resist the politicizing of their science.

Professionally, the spirit of Leopold and Ricketts is found in the natural history facts, techniques, and perspectives that form the foundation of the best of modern ecology. It is ingrained in the roots of environmentalism; both Leopold and Ricketts anticipated the environmental movement and New Age thinking, including the notions of deep ecology, ecological holism, and the Gaia hypothesis. It is found in the "-ologies" that ground the newer discipline of conservation biology—including mammalogy, ornithology, herpetology, ichthyology, invertebrate biology, parasitology, phycology, and botany (a field that somehow avoided nomenclatural convention). These are subjects that are being taught less and less often, or are being presented superficially, at a time when the world desperately needs the expertise embodied in their details.

The spirit of Leopold and Ricketts will not be found in a great deal of modern science. It will not be found in the minds of specialists. Nor is it in the minds of people centered on their careers. It will not be found in whiners or quitters. It will not be found in scientists who have grown old and tired, defensive, protective, and bitter. It is not in the minds of bureaucrats, especially those who take special joy in creating roadblocks to accomplishment. It does not reside in corporate junk science, or the "scientists" who profit from promoting the company line. It will not be found in the scientist whose first impulse following an achievement is to call a journalist. Dryballs (a favorite Ricketts term), one and all.

The spirit of Leopold and Ricketts is woven into the fabric of people who have, in the words of Paul Hawken, "an older grace and intelligence" that runs counter to our current obsession with ourselves, and the destructiveness that accompanies such short-sightedness.[2] Such grace and intelligence defines the children of Leopold and Ricketts.

Because the spirit of Leopold and Ricketts is found in facts— in inductive, bottom-up thinking—it is also found, by extension, in grass roots movements; in civil society and in citizen-based organizations formed in response to society's needs. In this way it provides a link between environmental justice and social justice. It is found in humble and respectful behavior, and in the reverse—people unafraid of authority. It permeates those with an "intelligent interest in the possibilities of living."[3] As Ricketts knew, it is the driving force behind many artists, musicians, and storytellers, and was found in Woody Guthrie, Steve Goodman, Mardy Murie, and Rachel Carson; it lives in and through their works. It is there in bottom-up recycling programs, organic farms, and local food initiatives. It may be born again in those evangelicals who are now prepared to protect creation.

It can be found in the most powerful idea of the twentieth century: the notion that economies and other societal behaviors must be driven by individuals and grounded in ecological principles if they are to be sustainable. This is the "key to the future" of humanity.

And what all this really says is that the spirit of Leopold and Ricketts is found in hope, in the simple joys of living, and in the possibilities that people provide for themselves in the finite system we call Earth—our home.

THE SHACK AND THE LAB

In Wisconsin a prairie fire dies out
People gather
In California the sun sets over a railroad track
Different people gather
They think they have found something
They are right
They think they are alone
They are wrong
Together they are stronger
Buildings, still standing, with doors wide open
Bear witness

NOTES

PREFACE

1. Susan F. Beegel, Susan Shillinglaw, and Wesley N. Tiffney Jr., eds., *Steinbeck and the Environment: Interdisciplinary Approaches* (Tuscaloosa: University of Alabama Press, 1997), 20.

2. I also selected them because they have been around me for a long time. In 1975, my freshman year at Iowa State, my English composition teacher was an elderly man who, on the first day of class, said, "You can write about anything that interests you. One of my best friends was Paul Errington, the world's expert on muskrats." Paul Errington was also the first leader of the first Fish and Wildlife Cooperative Unit, which J. N. "Ding" Darling set up at Iowa State University. Errington was Leopold's protégé (but was not, as is often claimed, his student). That was my indirect introduction to Leopold. Three years later, at the Iowa Lakeside Laboratory (where I was taking courses in buildings Ding Darling had the Milford Civilian Conservation Corps build in 1937), a graduate student, observing our social tendencies (which were probably no different from anyone else's at any other field station in any other time period), said, "They write books about what you guys do. Get Steinbeck's *Log*

from the Sea of Cortez and read about it." I did, and that was my introduction to Ricketts. I have a second connection to Ricketts. His favorite
teacher was W. C. Allee, who was the PhD adviser of my first mentor,
Dick Bovbjerg. As Richard Astro writes (*John Steinbeck and Edward F.
Ricketts: The Shaping of a Novelist* [Minneapolis: University of Minnesota Press, 1972], 5), "almost to a man Allee's students approached or
achieved greatness of mind. Probably a minute number of teachers have
ever so stimulated their students to think for themselves" (communication between Jack Calvin and Richard Astro, 7/4/69). This was certainly
true of Dick. Over the intervening thirty years I've accumulated all of
the significant books about Leopold and Ricketts.

3. Curt Meine, *Aldo Leopold: His Life and Work* (Madison: Univer-
sity of Wisconsin Press, 1988); Robert A. McCabe, *Aldo Leopold: The
Professor* (Madison, Wisc.: Palmer Publications, 1987); Tom Tanner, ed.,
Aldo Leopold: The Man and His Legacy (Ankeny, Iowa: Soil Conserva-
tion Society of America, 1987); J. Baird Callicott, *Companion to* A Sand
County Almanac: *Interpretive and Critical Essays* (Madison: University
of Wisconsin Press, 1987); Susan L. Flader, *Thinking like a Mountain:
Aldo Leopold and the Evolution of an Ecological Attitude toward Deer,
Wolves, and Forests* (Madison: University of Wisconsin Press, 1974).

4. Julianne Lutz Newton, *Aldo Leopold's Odyssey: Rediscovering the
Author of* A Sand County Almanac (Washington, D.C.: Island Press,
2006).

5. Astro, *Steinbeck and Ricketts;* Richard Astro, *Edward F. Ricketts,*
Western Writers Series 21 (Boise, Idaho: Boise State University, 1976).

6. Joel W. Hedgpeth, ed., *The Outer Shores,* pt. 1: *Ed Ricketts and
John Steinbeck Explore the Pacific Coast;* pt. 2: *Breaking Through* (Eureka, Calif.: Mad River Press, 1978); for "Doc," see John Steinbeck, *Cannery Row* (New York: Viking Press, 1945), and *Sweet Thursday* (New
York: Viking Press, 1954).

7. D. Burnor, "Ed Ricketts: From the Tidepools to the Stars," *CoEvo-
lution Quarterly* 28 (Winter 1980): 14–21.

8. Katie Rodger, *Renaissance Man of Cannery Row: The Life and
Letters of Edward F. Ricketts* (Tuscaloosa: University of Alabama Press,

2002), and *Breaking Through: Essays, Journals, and Travelogues of Edward F. Ricketts* (Berkeley: University of California Press, 2006).

9. Eric Enno Tamm, *Beyond the Outer Shores: The Untold Odyssey of Ed Ricketts, the Pioneering Ecologist Who Inspired John Steinbeck and Joseph Campbell* (New York: Thunder's Mouth Press, 2004).

10. Michael Lewis, *Moneyball: The Art of Winning an Unfair Game* (New York: W. W. Norton, 2003), 71.

INTRODUCTION

1. A detailed account of Leopold's last morning, including a portion of his daughter Estella's letter to Nina and a map indicating important aspects of the events of the fire, can be found in McCabe, *Aldo Leopold: Professor,* 142–45.

2. Curt mentioned this fascinating fact while we were eating pizza with Mike, Lisa, and Angus Mossman at a well-known establishment on the square in downtown Baraboo in August 2005, after an afternoon spent at the Shack and visiting Nina. I followed up on a snowy day in December 2007, when my family and I visited the library archives at the University of Wisconsin. There we met David Null, the director of the university archives, and he found for us archive no. 014, an open envelope measuring about five by six inches, labeled "Contents of A.L.'s Pocket upon his death." Inside was a smaller university envelope containing Leopold's driver's license, his insurance card (Provident Life and Accident Insurance Company), his University Club card, his University of Wisconsin faculty ID, his state ID, and a small picture of Estella, all charred except for the picture of Estella. The diary is the most damaged; in it is written on the first page, "Aldo Leopold 12/13/47–."

3. John Steinbeck, "About Ed Ricketts," in *The Log from the Sea of Cortez* (New York: Viking Press, 1951), 1.

4. I recognize how odd this phrasing must sound to the peoples of First Nations. I mean no insult and recognize that if their cultures had been allowed to flourish, and if they had been allowed to teach the immigrants coming from both coasts, there might not have been a need

for these early ecologists, and certainly there would not be the urgency surrounding environmental issues that we face today.

5. McCabe, *Aldo Leopold: Professor,* 165–66.

6. T. Perrottet, "John Muir's Yosemite," *Smithsonian* 39, no. 4 (April 2008): 48–55.

7. Personal communication, March 17, 2009.

8. Apsley Cherry-Garrard, *The Worst Journey in the World* (Washington, D.C.: National Geographic Society, 2002 [orig. 1922]), 201.

9. In a letter to Sparky Enea (one of the deckhands-cum-collectors on the *Western Flyer* during the Sea of Cortés trip) dated September 16, 1942, Ricketts wrote, "Roofers are working overhead. Got so we didn't have any comfortable place to sleep when it rained. About to ruin books, typewriters, etc. Things have gone up frightfully. This roof costs more than twice what the last one did" (Rodger, *Renaissance Man of Cannery Row,* 167). Leopold Shack journal, March 24, 1937, p. 18 (Aldo Leopold and his son Starker were visiting): "Drove through a biting blizzard and spent the afternoon chinking cracks to keep out the drifts, building clothes racks and other inside tinkering jobs."

10. Thanks to Eric Engles for his discussion of these differences.

11. Or maybe not so curious: see M. Gladwell, *Outliers: The Story of Success* (New York: Little, Brown, 2008). I am quoting Norman Maclean, "USFS 1919: The Ranger, the Cook, and a Hole in the Sky," in *A River Runs Through It and Other Stories* (Chicago: University of Chicago Press, 1976), 127.

12. Quoted in J. J. Benson, *John Steinbeck, Writer* (New York: Penguin Books, 1984), 431–32.

CHAPTER ONE

1. Meine, *Aldo Leopold,* 11, 17.

2. Rodger, *Renaissance Man of Cannery Row,* xv.

3. Meine, *Aldo Leopold,* 16.

4. Meine, *Aldo Leopold,* 18.

5. Meine, *Aldo Leopold,* 23–24.

6. Meine, *Aldo Leopold,* 24, from p. 6 of Frederic Leopold's reminiscence "Aldo's Middle School Years."

7. Meine, *Aldo Leopold,* 24.

8. Meine, *Aldo Leopold,* 35.

9. Rodger, *Renaissance Man of Cannery Row,* xv.

10. Rodger, *Renaissance Man of Cannery Row,* xv.

11. Letter from Ricketts to David M. Clay, in the editorial department at Harcourt, Brace (in Rodger, *Renaissance Man of Cannery Row,* 164–65).

12. Hedgpeth, ed., *The Outer Shores,* pt. 1, p. 3.

13. Rodger, *Renaissance Man of Cannery Row,* xvi, from p. 4 of Frances Strong's reminiscence.

14. Rodger, *Renaissance Man of Cannery Row,* xvi, from p. 4 of Frances Strong's reminiscence.

15. Rodger, *Renaissance Man of Cannery Row,* xvii.

16. Meine, *Aldo Leopold,* 25.

17. Rodger, *Renaissance Man of Cannery Row,* xiii; see also Benson, *John Steinbeck, Writer,* 560.

18. Meine, *Aldo Leopold,* 51.

19. Tanner, ed., *Aldo Leopold,* 5.

20. Meine, *Aldo Leopold,* 74.

21. Meine, *Aldo Leopold,* 80–81.

22. Rodger, *Renaissance Man of Cannery Row,* xvii.

23. Hedgpeth, ed., *The Outer Shores,* pt. 1, p. 4.

24. Steinbeck, *Cannery Row* (cited from the New York: Bantam Books edition, 1980), 64; see also Rodger, *Renaissance Man of Cannery Row,* xviii; and Benson, *John Steinbeck, Writer,* 190.

25. Hedgpeth, ed., *The Outer Shores,* pt. 1, p. 8.

26. Warder Clyde Allee, *Animal Aggregations: A Critical Study in General Sociology* (Chicago: University of Chicago Press, 1931).

27. Hedgpeth, ed., *The Outer Shores,* pt. 1, p. 5.

28. Hedgpeth, ed., *The Outer Shores,* pt. 1, p. 4; see also Rodger, *Renaissance Man of Cannery Row,* xxi.

29. Tanner, ed., *Aldo Leopold,* 5.

CHAPTER TWO

1. Meine, *Aldo Leopold,* 83.
2. Meine, *Aldo Leopold,* 93.
3. Meine, *Aldo Leopold,* 94.
4. Meine, *Aldo Leopold,* 121.
5. Meine, *Aldo Leopold,* 122–32.
6. Curt Meine, "The Farmer as Conservationist: Leopold on Agriculture," in Tanner, ed., *Aldo Leopold,* 40.
7. Meine, *Aldo Leopold,* 161.
8. Meine, *Aldo Leopold,* 163.
9. Meine, *Aldo Leopold,* 175.
10. Meine, *Aldo Leopold,* 198.
11. Meine, *Aldo Leopold,* 227.
12. Meine, *Aldo Leopold,* 225.
13. Meine, *Aldo Leopold,* 234.
14. Meine, *Aldo Leopold,* 247–48.
15. Meine, *Aldo Leopold,* 256.
16. Meine, *Aldo Leopold,* 256.
17. Meine, *Aldo Leopold,* 262.
18. Meine, *Aldo Leopold,* 263.
19. Meine, *Aldo Leopold,* 264.
20. Meine, *Aldo Leopold,* 266.
21. Meine, *Aldo Leopold,* 274.
22. Meine, *Aldo Leopold,* 278; R. A. Leopold, *Report on a Game Survey of the North Central States* (Madison, Wisc.: The Democrat Press for the Sporting Arms and Ammunition Manufacturers' Institute, 1931).
23. Meine, *Aldo Leopold,* 279.
24. Meine, *Aldo Leopold,* 280.
25. Meine, *Aldo Leopold,* 280.

CHAPTER THREE

1. Hedgpeth, ed., *The Outer Shores,* pt. 1, pp. 1–2.
2. Tamm, *Beyond the Outer Shores,* 10.

3. W.C. Allee, "Studies in Marine Ecology: I. The Distribution of Common Littoral Invertebrates of the Woods Hole Region," *Biological Bulletin* 18 (1923): 167–91; and "Some Physical Factors Related to the Distribution of Littoral Invertebrates," *Biological Bulletin* 18 (1923): 205–53.

4. Hedgpeth, ed., *The Outer Shores,* pt. 1, p. 6.

5. Steinbeck, *Log from the Sea of Cortez,* xvii.

6. Hedgpeth, ed., *The Outer Shores,* pt. 1, p. 10.

7. Quoted in Hedgpeth, ed., *The Outer Shores,* pt. 1, p. 8.

8. By all accounts Carol Steinbeck was a remarkable person, with a quick, sharp wit. She was one of several in the Lab group known as "termites," a group of gifted and talented children, near geniuses, on whom Luis Terman, the Stanford psychologist who studied intelligence, had initiated a lifelong study. It was Carol's idea to name her husband's most famous novel *The Grapes of Wrath* (S. Larsen and R. Larsen, *Joseph Campbell: A Fire in the Mind* [Rochester, Vt.: Inner Traditions, 1991], 182). For more about Luis Terman and his termites, see J.N. Shurkin, *Terman's Kids: The Groundbreaking Study of How the Gifted Grow Up* (New York: Little, Brown, 1992), and Gladwell, *Outliers,* chap. 3.

9. Steinbeck told a different story, describing a first meeting in the waiting room of a dentist's office in "About Ed Ricketts." But according to Hedgpeth (*The Outer Shores,* pt. 1, p. 10), both Steinbeck's and Ricketts's wives of that time remember them meeting at Calvin's house. Ed's sister, Frances Strong, remembers the incident at the dentist's office, without the embellishment.

10. Astro, *Steinbeck and Ricketts.*

11. Rodger, *Renaissance Man of Cannery Row,* xxiv.

12. Rodger, *Renaissance Man of Cannery Row,* xxiv; from E. Steinbeck and R. Wallsten, *Steinbeck: A Life in Letters* (New York: Viking Press, 1975), 295–96.

13. Astro, *Steinbeck and Ricketts,* 67.

14. Quoted in Hedgpeth, ed., *The Outer Shores,* pt. 2, p. 162; Rodger, *Renaissance Man of Cannery Row,* xxv.

15. Tamm, *Beyond the Outer Shores,* 11–13.

16. *Flivver* was a common term in the 1920s and 1930s for inexpensive automobiles (see also Aldo S. Leopold, *A Sand County Almanac and Sketches Here and There* [New York: Oxford University Press, 1949], 217). And there seemed to be some passion for giving them names. Joseph Grinnell, the first director of the Natural History Museum at the University of California, Berkeley, had a Ford he called Perodipus, which he used on his collecting trips. According to Robert E. Kohler, "Not any auto would do for cross country travel. Fords were a good choice for rough fieldwork—the only choice, Joseph Grinnell thought, because they were designed for farm use and do-it-yourself repair. For very rough country they were fitted out with heavy-duty springs and plenty of spare tires and other parts" (*All Creatures: Naturalists, Collectors, and Biodiversity, 1850–1950* [Princeton, N.J.: Princeton University Press, 2006], 166–67).

17. Larsen and Larsen, *Joseph Campbell,* 189–90.

18. Thanks to Shelly Grow for this observation.

19. Tamm, *Beyond the Outer Shores,* 13.

20. Tamm, *Beyond the Outer Shores,* 13; N. Eldredge and S. J. Gould, "Punctuated Equilibria: An Alternative to Phyletic Gradualism," in T. J. M. Schopf, ed., *Models in Paleobiology* (San Francisco: Freeman Cooper, 1972), 82–115.

21. Tamm, *Beyond the Outer Shores,* 13.

22. Quoted in Rodger, *Renaissance Man of Cannery Row,* 205.

23. Larsen and Larsen, *Joseph Campbell,* 206.

24. Benson, *John Steinbeck, Writer,* 181.

25. Benson, *John Steinbeck, Writer,* 232.

26. Quoted in Larsen and Larsen, *Joseph Campbell,* 175.

27. Tamm, *Beyond the Outer Shores,* 14–15.

28. Tamm, *Beyond the Outer Shores,* 185–88.

29. Tamm, *Beyond the Outer Shores,* 189.

30. Tamm, *Beyond the Outer Shores,* 189.

31. Tamm, *Beyond the Outer Shores,* 185.

32. Larsen and Larsen, *Joseph Campbell,* 204.

33. Tamm, *Beyond the Outer Shores,* 180.

34. Quoted in Tamm, *Beyond the Outer Shores,* 17.

CHAPTER FOUR

1. Meine, *Aldo Leopold,* 278.
2. Meine, *Aldo Leopold,* 281.
3. Meine, *Aldo Leopold,* 284.
4. Meine, *Aldo Leopold,* 285.
5. Meine, *Aldo Leopold,* 285.
6. Olaus J. Murie, *Peterson Field Guides: Animal Tracks* (New York: Houghton Mifflin, 1954).
7. Quoted in Meine, *Aldo Leopold,* 287.
8. Quoted in Meine, *Aldo Leopold,* 288.
9. Aldo Leopold, *Game Management* (Madison: University of Wisconsin Press, 1986 [orig. New York: Charles Scribner's Sons, 1933]), 230.
10. Meine, *Aldo Leopold,* 293.
11. Leopold, *Game Management,* 423.

CHAPTER FIVE

1. Rodger, *Renaissance Man of Cannery Row,* 38–39; quotation from a letter from Ricketts to Virginia Scardigli, April 25, 1939.
2. Rodger, *Renaissance Man of Cannery Row,* xxx.
3. Rodger, *Breaking Through,* 12.
4. On Verrill and Smith, see Hedgpeth, ed., *The Outer Shores,* pt. 1, p. 25.
5. Quoted in Tamm, *Beyond the Outer Shores,* 92.
6. Edward F. Ricketts, EFR Essay no. 2, Ts. Edward F. Ricketts Papers, M0291, Special Collections, Stanford University Library, Stanford, California. Thanks to Katie Rodger for providing this reference.
7. Hedgpeth, ed., *The Outer Shores,* pt. 1, pp. 24–25.
8. Tamm, *Beyond the Outer Shores,* 28–29.
9. Rodger, *Breaking Through,* 18.
10. Hedgpeth, ed., *The Outer Shores,* pt. 1, p. 14.
11. Quoted in Hedgpeth, ed., *The Outer Shores,* pt. 1, pp. 25–28.
12. Edward F. Ricketts and Jack Calvin, *Between Pacific Tides* (Stan-

ford, Calif.: Stanford University Press, 1939). I own and have consulted two subsequent editions: the revised, 1948, edition, which Ricketts completed just before he died, and the 4th edition, revised by Joel Hedgpeth and published in 1968.

13. Quoted in Rodger, *Renaissance Man of Cannery Row,* 34.

14. Quoted in Rodger, *Renaissance Man of Cannery Row,* 38–39.

15. Tamm, *Beyond the Outer Shores,* 32.

CHAPTER SIX

1. Meine, *Aldo Leopold,* 307. According to Bob McCabe (*Aldo Leopold: Professor,* 11), Leopold impressed University of Wisconsin dean Harry L. Russell and other members of the Getaway Club, a group of men who met to present papers on outdoor, historical, and travel experiences.

2. M. Lorbiecki, *Aldo Leopold: A Fierce Green Fire* (Helena and Billings, Mont.: Falcon Publishing, 1996), 123.

3. Stephen Jay Gould, *An Urchin in the Storm* (New York: W. W. Norton, 1983), 79.

4. Nina Leopold Bradley, "A Daughter's Reflections," in Lorbiecki, *Aldo Leopold,* 185–86.

5. See, for example, Stephen Jay Gould's essay "The Panda's Thumb" in his book of the same name (New York: W. W. Norton, 1980).

6. Meine, *Aldo Leopold,* 340.

7. Meine, *Aldo Leopold,* 340–41; Shack journal, vol. 1, p. 1. Ed Ochsner was a remarkable man, a fur buyer, taxidermist, and beekeeper who worked in and around Baraboo, including for Alfred Ringling and the Ringling Brothers, Barnum and Bailey Circus (see H. L. Stoddard, *Memoirs of a Naturalist* [Norman: University of Oklahoma Press, 1969], for more details).

8. Nina Leopold Bradley, quoted in Tanner, ed., *Aldo Leopold,* 170–71. There is some confusion about whether the family first saw the Shack, in 1935 or 1936. On May 14, 2008, I e-mailed Curt Meine, "In Tom Tanner's book, p. 170, Nina writes that the whole family saw the Shack for the first time in Feb. 1936, but there is no 1936 Shack entry until March 1.

There is a Feb. entry for 1935. Do you think Nina's 1936 is the wrong date (that it was 1935), or that Nina's Feb. is the wrong month (that it was really March). For March 7 and 8th, 1936, 'Whole family' is written." Curt replied, "My guess is that Nina (or the editors!) had the year mistaken, and the Feb. 1935 date is the right one. There were differences in the memories of the children about their first visit(s). After interviewing the four surviving children separately, I had four divergent accounts! When I had them all together and explained, they threw their hands up and asked me to just use my best judgment from the evidence!"

9. In Lorbiecki, *Aldo Leopold,* 185–86.

10. Meine, *Aldo Leopold,* 392.

11. Meine, *Aldo Leopold,* 391–92.

12. The Shack journals are housed in the archives of the University of Wisconsin Library. They may also be accessed online at http:// images.library.wisc.edu. Go to UWDC Digital Collections: Diaries and Journals: Shack Journals.

13. In the best tradition of Leopold's data analysis, I compiled the dates when the journals indicated the Shack was occupied. I then used these data to plot the number of days visited (figure 1) and number of trips per year (figure 2). Dividing the first by the second, I arrived at the mean number of days per visit (figure 3). These data must be considered approximate. There are several possible errors in this analysis. First, it is certain that not every day at the Shack has a journal entry. During the 1936 Christmas holidays the family visited the Shack for four days and left no record in the journal (Leopold wrote elsewhere [Meine, *Aldo Leopold,* 370], "Too good a time to make note in journal"). This is probably also the case when a string of days present is interrupted by a single day absent and is followed by a string of days present; examples include June 11–19, 1939, and August 10–14, 1940. Second, there are places where the entries themselves are inaccurate. For example, the subheading "Weather" on December 14–15 1946, is dated "11/14"; and February 29–March 2, 1947, cannot be correct, since 1947 was not a leap year. The third source of error is my own. Although I combed through these journals several times, reading both hard copy and digital copy, I suspect I've made mistakes.

14. Bradley, in Tanner, ed., *Aldo Leopold,* 170–71.

15. But as Meine points out (*Aldo Leopold,* 412), winter trips to the Shack were especially enjoyable because signs in the snow recorded animal activities, and in particular the high drama of predator-prey interactions.

16. Meine, *Aldo Leopold,* 398.

17. Meine, *Aldo Leopold,* 440.

18. Meine, *Aldo Leopold,* 440, 447, 466.

19. See also Meine, *Aldo Leopold,* 484.

CHAPTER SEVEN

1. Hedgpeth, ed., *The Outer Shores,* pt. 1, pp. 1–2.

2. Bruce Ariss, *Inside Cannery Row: Sketches from the Steinbeck Era* (Nevada City, Calif.: Lexikos, 1988), 23–24.

3. Hedgpeth, ed., *The Outer Shores,* pt. 1, p. 6.

4. Benson, *John Steinbeck, Writer,* 193.

5. Rodger, *Breaking Through,* 9.

6. In Bruce Ariss's mural in the Monterey Bay Aquarium, however, the prefire Lab at 800 Ocean View Avenue is sandwiched between the San Carlos Canning Company and the Monterey Canning Company.

7. Commentary contained in California Views: The Pat Hathaway Photo Collection, found at http://www.caviews.com/ricketts.htm, accessed April 23, 2008.

8. Quoted in Rodger, *Breaking Through,* 9.

9. Quoted in Rodger, *Breaking Through,* 9.

10. Ariss, *Inside Cannery Row,* 3.

11. Tamm, *Beyond the Outer Shores,* 5.

12. Ariss, *Inside Cannery Row,* 13.

13. Ariss, *Inside Cannery Row,* 6.

14. Steinbeck, *Cannery Row,* 15–16; Benson, *John Steinbeck, Writer,* 195–96.

15. Ariss, *Inside Cannery Row,* 26.

16. John Steinbeck, *Travels with Charley* (New York: Viking Penguin, 1962; reissued by Penguin in paperback, 1986), 209.

17. Quoted in Benson, *John Steinbeck, Writer,* 252–54.

18. Steinbeck, *Log from the Sea of Cortez,* xv.

19. Tamm, *Beyond the Outer Shores,* 30.

20. Ariss, *Inside Cannery Row,* 81–82.

21. Quoted in Rodger, *Renaissance Man of Cannery Row,* 1–2.

22. Benson, *John Steinbeck, Writer,* 196.

23. Tamm, *Beyond the Outer Shores,* 146–49.

24. Quoted in Rodger, *Renaissance Man of Cannery Row,* 9–10.

25. Quoted in Rodger, *Renaissance Man of Cannery Row,* 11.

26. Quoted in Rodger, *Renaissance Man of Cannery Row,* 12–13.

27. Quoted in Rodger, *Renaissance Man of Cannery Row,* 25.

28. Quoted in Rodger, *Renaissance Man of Cannery Row,* 28–29.

29. Hedgpeth (*The Outer Shores,* pt. 1, p. 42) says de Roos worked for the *San Francisco Chronicle,* which, indeed, is where he began. de Roos was an award-winning journalist who later worked for many magazines over his illustrious career, including *Life, Sports Illustrated,* and *National Geographic.*

30. Quoted in Rodger, *Renaissance Man of Cannery Row,* 210.

31. Quoted in Hedgpeth, ed., *The Outer Shores,* pt. 1, p. 42.

32. Ariss, *Inside Cannery Row,* 14.

33. Benson, *John Steinbeck, Writer,* 225.

34. Benson, *John Steinbeck, Writer,* 227–28.

35. Benson, *John Steinbeck, Writer,* 225, 228.

36. Benson, *John Steinbeck, Writer,* 435.

37. Quoted in Rodger, *Renaissance Man of Cannery Row,* 138–39.

38. Tamm, *Beyond the Outer Shores,* 144.

39. Rodger, *Renaissance Man of Cannery Row,* xlvii.

40. Steinbeck and Wallsten, *Steinbeck: A Life in Letters,* 295–96.

CHAPTER EIGHT

1. Meine, *Aldo Leopold,* 416–17.

2. In Meine's essay "Moving Mountains," contained in his book *Correction Lines* (Washington, D.C.: Island Press, 2004), he chronicles

the story of how *A Sand County Almanac* came together. In addition to providing a fascinating narrative, Meine sets out a chronology of the key events involved in its assembly and publication. For folks interested in how talent and serendipity align to produce a classic, I highly recommend this essay (and, in fact, Curt's book).

3. Meine, *Aldo Leopold,* 419.

4. Meine, *Aldo Leopold,* 447.

5. Meine, *Aldo Leopold,* 453.

6. Quoted in Meine, *Aldo Leopold,* 453–54.

7. Meine, *Aldo Leopold,* 458.

8. Meine, *Aldo Leopold,* 459.

9. Quoted in Meine, *Aldo Leopold,* 460.

10. Quoted in Meine, *Aldo Leopold,* 460–61.

11. Meine, *Aldo Leopold,* 485.

12. Meine, *Aldo Leopold,* 486.

13. Meine, *Aldo Leopold,* 500–501.

14. Meine, *Aldo Leopold,* 507.

15. Meine, *Aldo Leopold,* 509–10.

16. For the best angry letter written to Alfred A. Knopf for rejecting a book manuscript, we roll the clock forward forty-one years to the 1988 letter Norman Maclean wrote in response to Knopf's solicitation of Maclean's second book, *Young Men and Fire,* after the firm had rejected his first book, *A River Runs through It and Other Essays* (but not before, according to Maclean, they played "games with it, or at least the game of cat's-paw, now rolling it over and saying they were going to publish it and then rolling it on its back when the president of the company announced it wouldn't sell"). This letter has become an underground classic, and now appears on several personal Web sites. Imagine the profits Knopf would have realized had they published both *A Sand County Almanac* and *A River Runs through It.* But despite these misses, Knopf has had its share of hits, including Mardy Murie's 1957 classic *Two in the Far North.* There must be many head-banging uncertainties associated with predicting the commercial success of books.

17. Meine, *Aldo Leopold,* 510.

18. Meine, *Aldo Leopold,* 517.

19. On the boy friend, see McCabe, *Aldo Leopold: Professor,* 142.

20. Meine, *Aldo Leopold,* 524.

21. Meine, *Aldo Leopold,* 524.

22. Meine, *Aldo Leopold,* 524.

23. Aldo S. Leopold, *A Sand County Almanac and Sketches Here and There* (New York: Oxford University Press, 1949).

24. Bradley, in Tanner, ed., *Aldo Leopold,* 173–74.

CHAPTER NINE

1. John Steinbeck, *The Grapes of Wrath* (New York: Viking Press, 1939).

2. R. DeMott, ed., *Working Days: The Journals of The Grapes of Wrath* (New York: Penguin Books, 1989), 106; also Rodger, *Renaissance Man of Cannery Row,* xxxvii.

3. Benson, *John Steinbeck, Writer,* 428.

4. Quoted in Rodger, *Renaissance Man of Cannery Row,* xxxix.

5. Benson, *John Steinbeck, Writer,* 427–28; Steinbeck and Wallsten, *Steinbeck: A Life in Letters,* 184.

6. Benson, *John Steinbeck, Writer,* 428.

7. Rodger, *Breaking Through,* 34–35.

8. Rodger, *Breaking Through,* 34.

9. In a letter to Herb and Rosa Kline, March 7, 1940; Rodger, *Renaissance Man of Cannery Row,* 57.

10. Benson, *John Steinbeck, Writer,* 444–45.

11. Rodger, *Breaking Through,* 37.

12. Benson, *John Steinbeck, Writer,* 440.

13. Benson, *John Steinbeck, Writer,* 440.

14. Rodger, *Renaissance Man of Cannery Row,* xl–xli.

15. Rodger, *Breaking Through,* 40.

16. John Steinbeck and E. F. Ricketts, *Sea of Cortez: A Leisurely Journal of Travel and Research* (New York: Viking Press, 1941). My copy is a facsimile edition (Mamaroneck, N.Y.: Paul R. Appel, 1971).

17. Astro, *Steinbeck and Ricketts,* 136; see also Rodger, *Breaking Through,* 42.

18. Letter to Rich and Tal Lovejoy, June 18, 1940, in Rodger, *Renaissance Man of Cannery Row,* 59–61.

19. Rodger, *Renaissance Man of Cannery Row,* xliii, cites "Second 1940, Notebook One."

20. Letter to Rich and Tal Lovejoy, June 1940, in Rodger, *Renaissance Man of Cannery Row,* 61–65.

21. Rodger, *Renaissance Man of Cannery Row,* xliv.

22. DeMott, ed., *Working Days,* 125–26.

23. Steinbeck and Wallsten, *Steinbeck: A Life in Letters,* 214.

24. Steinbeck and Wallsten, *Steinbeck: A Life in Letters,* 213.

25. Seixas Solomons; Jackson was her pen name. Her father, Theodore Seixas Solomons, explored the Sierra Nevada in the late nineteenth century, was a founding member of the Sierra Club, and mapped the route that would become the John Muir Trail (Rodger, *Renaissance Man of Cannery Row,* 149). See also S. Sargent, *Solomons of the Sierra* (Yosemite, Calif.: Flying Spur Press, 1989); thanks to Katie Rodger for suggesting this book.

26. Rodger, *Breaking Through,* 46.

27. Steinbeck and Ricketts, *Sea of Cortez,* 284.

28. Steinbeck and Wallsten, *Steinbeck: A Life in Letters,* 216–17.

29. Steinbeck and Wallsten, *Steinbeck: A Life in Letters,* 217.

30. Rodger, *Renaissance Man of Cannery Row,* 118.

31. Steinbeck and Wallsten, *Steinbeck: A Life in Letters,* 223; Rodger, *Renaissance Man of Cannery Row,* xlv.

32. Rodger, *Renaissance Man of Cannery Row,* xlvi.

CHAPTER TEN

1. Leopold was familiar with Allee and his work. In fact, his daughter Nina worked for Allee during the early 1940s. Further, both Leopold and Ricketts corresponded with Joseph Grinnell at Berkeley. Starker Leopold studied with Grinnell when he was working toward his PhD.

2. Meine, *Aldo Leopold,* 25.

3. Meine, *Aldo Leopold,* 389.

4. Benson, *John Steinbeck, Writer,* 197.

5. Benson, *John Steinbeck, Writer,* 198.

6. Hedgpeth, ed., *The Outer Shores,* pt. 2, p. 21.

7. Benson, *John Steinbeck, Writer,* 183.

8. Leopold, *Sand County Almanac,* 187.

9. Benson, *John Steinbeck, Writer,* 187.

10. Benson, *John Steinbeck, Writer,* 190.

11. Kurt Vonnegut, *Man without a Country* (New York: Random House, 2007), 20.

12. Benson, *John Steinbeck, Writer,* 190.

13. Conversation between Joel Hedgpeth and Richard Astro, July 15, 1970, in Astro, *Steinbeck and Ricketts,* 25.

14. Hedgpeth, ed., *The Outer Shores,* pt. 1, pp. 8–10.

15. Hedgpeth, ed., *The Outer Shores,* pt. 1, p. 6.

16. Benson, *John Steinbeck, Writer,* 195.

17. Rodger, *Renaissance Man of Cannery Row,* 138–39.

CHAPTER ELEVEN

1. F. Capra and D. Steindl-Rast, *Belonging to the Universe* (San Francisco: Harper and Row, 1991), 85, cited in J.C. Kelly, "John Steinbeck and Ed Ricketts: Understanding Life in the Great Tide Pool," in Beegel, Shillinglaw, and Tiffney, eds., *Steinbeck and the Environment,* 27–42.

2. Benson, *John Steinbeck, Writer,* 431–32.

3. Kohler, *All Creatures,* 270; see also D. Worster, *Nature's Economy: A History of Ecological Ideas,* 2nd ed. (New York: Cambridge University Press, 1994).

4. Kohler, *All Creatures,* xi.

5. Kohler, *All Creatures,* 50.

6. Kohler, *All Creatures,* 64–65.

7. Kohler, *All Creatures,* 70–71.

8. Kohler, *All Creatures,* 94.

9. Kohler, *All Creatures,* 75.

10. Kohler, *All Creatures,* 135.

11. Kohler, *All Creatures,* 2.

12. C. Bergmann, "Über die Verhältnisse der Wärmeökonomie der Thiere zu ihere Grösse," *Göttinger Studien* 3 (1847): 595–708; J. A. Allen, "The Influence of Physical Conditions in the Genesis of Species," *Radical Review* 1 (1877): 108–40.

13. Howard Gardner, *Changing Minds: The Art and Science of Changing Our Own and Other People's Minds* (Cambridge, Mass.: Harvard Business School Press, 2006), 193.

14. Kohler, *All Creatures,* 210.

15. H. L. Stoddard, *Memoirs of a Naturalist* (Norman: University of Oklahoma Press, 1969).

16. Leopold, *Sand County Almanac,* 203–04.

17. Meine, *Aldo Leopold,* 395–96.

18. Meine, *Aldo Leopold,* 395–96.

19. Meine, *Aldo Leopold,* 395.

20. Leopold, *Sand County Almanac,* 189.

21. Quoted in Larsen and Larsen, *Joseph Campbell,* 202.

22. Timothy Egan, *The Worst Hard Time* (New York: Mariner Books, Houghton Mifflin, 2006), 51.

23. Egan, *The Worst Hard Time,* 175.

24. Egan, *The Worst Hard Time,* 221.

25. Egan, *The Worst Hard Time,* 150.

26. Egan, *The Worst Hard Time,* 138.

27. Egan, *The Worst Hard Time,* 153.

28. Egan, *The Worst Hard Time,* 256.

29. Egan, *The Worst Hard Time,* 227.

30. Egan, *The Worst Hard Time,* 225.

31. Egan, *The Worst Hard Time,* 228.

32. Egan, *The Worst Hard Time,* 226.

33. Egan, *The Worst Hard Time,* 169.

CHAPTER TWELVE

1. In Lorbiecki, *Aldo Leopold,* 185–86.

2. Quoted in Egan, *The Worst Hard Time,* 125.

3. Egan, *The Worst Hard Time,* 134.

4. Aldo Leopold, "Land Pathology," address to the University of Wisconsin chapter of Sigma Xi, April 14, 1935; Meine, *Aldo Leopold,* 405.

5. Quoted in Meine, *Aldo Leopold,* 368.

6. Aldo Leopold, "Biotic View of Land," address to a joint meeting of American Foresters and the Ecological Society of America, June 21, 1939; Meine, *Aldo Leopold,* 404.

7. Writings on the subject include R. M. May, *Stability and Complexity in Model Ecosystems* (Princeton, N.J.: Princeton University Press, 1973); S. Pimm, "The Complexity and Stability of Ecosystems," *Nature* 307 (1984): 321–26; D. Tilman, J. Knops, D. Wedin, P. Reich, M. Richie, and E. Siemann, "The Influence of Functional Diversity and Composition on Ecosystem Processes," *Science* 277 (1997): 1300–1302; D. Tilman, "The Ecological Consequences of Changes in Biodiversity: A Search for General Principles," *Ecology* 80 (1999): 1455–74; K. S. McCann, "The Diversity-Stability Debate," *Nature* 405 (2000): 228–33; B. Worm and J. E. Duffy, "Biodiversity, Productivity and Stability in Real Food Webs," *Trends in Ecology and Evolution* 18 (2003): 628–32.

8. Meine, *Aldo Leopold,* 404.

9. Quoted in Meine, *Aldo Leopold,* 465.

10. Quoted in Meine, *Aldo Leopold,* 349–50.

11. Quoted in Meine, *Aldo Leopold,* 414.

12. Quoted in Meine, *Aldo Leopold,* 404.

13. Quoted in Meine, *Aldo Leopold,* 415.

14. Meine, *Aldo Leopold,* 430–31.

15. Quoted in Meine, *Aldo Leopold,* 498.

16. Meine, *Aldo Leopold,* 499.

17. Aldo Leopold, "The Ecological Conscience," address deliv-

ered to the Conservation Committee of the Garden Club of America on June 27, 1947, in Minneapolis, Minnesota; Meine, *Aldo Leopold,* 497–98.

18. Meine, *Aldo Leopold,* 500; italics original.

19. Meine, *Aldo Leopold,* 350.

20. Presented as the John Wesley Powell lecture to the Southwest Division of the American Association for the Advancement of Science in Las Cruces, New Mexico, 1933; Meine, *Aldo Leopold,* 302, 350.

21. Leopold, *Sand County Almanac,* 262.

22. Lewis, *Moneyball,* 191.

23. Tamm, *Beyond the Outer Shores,* 102.

CHAPTER THIRTEEN

1. J. B. Callicott, "Turning the Whole Soul: The Educational Dialectic of 'A Sand County Almanac,'" *Worldviews* 9 (2005): 365–84. Many thanks to Nina Leopold Bradley for sending me a copy of this paper.

2. Astro, *Steinbeck and Ricketts,* 28.

3. Quoted in Meine, *Aldo Leopold,* 413–14.

4. Hedgpeth, ed., *The Outer Shores,* pt. 1, p. 81.

5. Hedgpeth, ed., *The Outer Shores,* pt. 2, p. 59.

6. Astro, *Steinbeck and Ricketts,* 35.

7. E. F. Ricketts, "The Philosophy of 'Breaking Through,'" revised July 1940 in Mexico City. Unpublished in Ricketts's lifetime; found in Hedgpeth, ed., *The Outer Shores,* pt. 2, pp. 69–79, and in Rodger, *Breaking Through,* 90–104.

8. Astro, *Steinbeck and Ricketts,* 37–38.

9. Astro, *Steinbeck and Ricketts,* 38–39. Published as chapter 14: "March 24, Easter Sunday," in Steinbeck and Ricketts, *Sea of Cortez,* 131–51.

10. Astro, *Steinbeck and Ricketts,* 39.

11. Rodger, *Renaissance Man of Cannery Row,* xxxiii.

12. Quoted in Rodger, *Renaissance Man of Cannery Row,* 43. "The

Spiritual Morphology of Poetry," unpublished in Ricketts's lifetime, may be found in Hedgpeth, ed., *The Outer Shores,* pt. 2, pp. 80–89 and in Rodger, *Breaking Through,* 106–18.

13. Rodger, *Renaissance Man of Cannery Row,* xxxiii.

14. Benson, *John Steinbeck, Writer,* 555.

15. Tamm, *Beyond the Outer Shores,* 136.

16. Astro, *Steinbeck and Ricketts,* 39.

17. Astro, *Steinbeck and Ricketts,* 41.

18. Steinbeck and Ricketts, *Sea of Cortez,* 257.

19. J. Lehrer, "The Eureka Hunt," *The New Yorker* (July 28, 2008): 40–45. Many thanks to Warren Vander Hill for calling this article to my attention. M. Jung-Beeman, E. M. Bowden, J. Haberman, J. L. Frymiare, S. Arambel-Liu, R. Greenblatt, P. J. Reber, and J. Kounios, "Neural Activity Observed in People Solving Verbal Problems with Insight," *Public Library of Science—Biology* 2 (2004): 500–510; J. Kounios, J. L. Frymiare, E. M. Bowden, J. I. Fleck, K. Subramaniam, T. B. Parrish, and M. Jung-Beeman, "The Prepared Mind: Neural Activity Prior to Problem Presentation Predicts Solution by Sudden Insight," *Psychological Science* 17 (2006): 882–90.

20. Rodger, *Breaking Through,* 325–30.

21. Rafe Sagarin and Larry B. Crowder, "Breaking through the Crisis in Marine Conservation and Management: Insights from the Philosophies of Ed Ricketts," *Conservation Biology* 23 (2009): 24–30.

CHAPTER FOURTEEN

1. Katie Rodger, personal communication, October 5, 2008.

2. Astro, *Steinbeck and Ricketts,* 8; Hedgpeth, ed., *The Outer Shores,* pt. 1, pp. 40–41.

3. Quoted in Meine, *Aldo Leopold,* 482–83.

4. Meine, *Aldo Leopold,* 415.

5. Quoted in Meine, *Aldo Leopold,* 490.

6. Meine, *Aldo Leopold,* 490.

7. Steinbeck, *Log from the Sea of Cortez,* 5.

8. Astro, *Steinbeck and Ricketts,* 29; italics original. In a strict sense, *organon* derives from Aristotle and comprises a set of logical principles. Astro seems to use it here to reflect holistic knowledge, as in a "sense of the organic."

9. Astro, *Steinbeck and Ricketts,* 29.

10. Meine, *Aldo Leopold,* 348.

11. Personal communication, March 17, 2009.

12. E.F. Ricketts, EFR Essay no. 2, Ts. Edward F. Ricketts Papers, M0291, Special Collections, Stanford University Library, Stanford, California. Thanks to Katie Rodger for providing this reference.

13. Quoted in Meine, *Aldo Leopold,* 235.

14. Hedgpeth, ed., *The Outer Shores,* pt. 1, p. 74.

15. Meine, *Aldo Leopold,* 376.

16. Tamm, *Beyond the Outer Shores,* 172.

17. Tamm, *Beyond the Outer Shores,* 171.

18. Tamm, *Beyond the Outer Shores,* 238.

19. Tamm, *Beyond the Outer Shores,* 239.

20. Meine, *Aldo Leopold,* 456.

21. In an e-mail dated December 6, 2008 written in response to a letter I sent asking him about the incident. Throughout this project, the Leopolds have been extraordinarily gracious and generous with their time and their stories.

22. Meine, *Aldo Leopold,* 470.

23. Quoted in Rodger, *Renaissance Man of Cannery Row,* 181.

24. Quoted in Rodger, *Renaissance Man of Cannery Row,* 190–91.

25. Quoted in Meine, *Aldo Leopold,* 473.

26. Hedgpeth, ed., *The Outer Shores,* pt. 1, p. 61.

INTERCALARY IV

1. Personal communication, March 17, 2009.

2. Steven G. Herman, "Wildlife Biology and Natural History: Time

for a Reunion," *Journal of Wildlife Management* 66 (2002): 933–46. Thanks to Eric Engles for this citation.

3. Herman, "Wildlife Biology," 934.

4. Paul K. Dayton, "Why Nature at the University of California?" *The NRS Transect* 26, no. 2 (2008): 7–14. Thanks to Eric Engles for this citation.

CHAPTER FIFTEEN

1. Meine, *Aldo Leopold,* 522.

2. Tamm, *Beyond the Outer Shores,* 271–72.

3. McCabe, *Aldo Leopold: Professor,* 145.

4. Benson, *John Steinbeck, Writer,* 615.

5. C. C. Bradley, "The Leopold Memorial Reserve," in Tanner, ed., *Aldo Leopold,* 162. Bradley is Nina Leopold's husband.

6. Lorbiecki, *Aldo Leopold,* 182.

7. Meine, personal communication, December 2007.

8. Ariss, *Inside Cannery Row,* 107.

9. Ed B. Larsh, *Doc's Lab: Myth and Legends of Cannery Row* (Monterey, Calif.: PBL Press, 1997), 79, 86, 88. This is a quirky stream-of-consciousness book, written by one of the artists who inhabited Ricketts's Lab after he died, about the other artists in the group. I've never seen this work cited by any other author, and say, "Thank dee lawd" for online search engines and booksellers who post their inventory.

10. Larsh, *Doc's Lab,* 88.

11. Ariss, *Inside Cannery Row,* 107.

12. Larsh, *Doc's Lab,* 128.

13. Hedgpeth, ed., *The Outer Shores,* pt. 2, p. 62.

14. http://www.93950.com/steinbeck/ricketts.htm, accessed March 1, 2009.

15. http://www.mbari.org, accessed March 1, 2009. Thanks to Vance Vredenberg for the heads-up.

16. R. D. Sagarin, W. F. Gilly, C. H. Baxter, N. Burnett, and J. Christensen, "Remembering the Gulf: Changes to the Marine Communi-

ties of the Sea of Cortez since the Steinbeck and Ricketts Expedition of 1940," *Frontiers in Ecology* 6 (2008): 372–79.

17. Bradley, "The Leopold Memorial Reserve," in Tanner, ed., *Aldo Leopold,* 163.

18. Geoffrey Dunn, Sheet Metal Memories, accessed at http://www.metroactive.com/metro/07.19.06ed-ricketts-0629.html on March 23, 2008.

CHAPTER SIXTEEN

1. Michael Pollan, *The Omnivore's Dilemma* (New York: Penguin Books, 2006), 260.

2. Herman E. Daly, *Beyond Growth: The Economics of Sustainable Development* (Boston, Mass.: Beacon Press, 1996). Many thanks to Shelly Grow for pointing me toward Daly's work.

3. C.G. Jung, *Collected Works,* vol. 5: *Symbols of Transformation,* trans. R.F.C. Hull (New York and London: 1911–12, rev. by Jung in 1952); cited in D. Backes, *A Wilderness Within: The Life of Sigurd F. Olson* (Minneapolis: University of Minnesota Press, 1997), 151.

4. Stephen Jay Gould, *Leonardo's Mountain of Clams and the Diet of Worms* (New York: Three Rivers Press, 1998), 262.

5. Steinbeck and Ricketts, *Sea of Cortez,* 96.

6. Michael Pollan, *Botany of Desire* (New York: Random House, 2001), xvi.

7. Steinbeck, *Sweet Thursday,* 159.

8. Steinbeck and Wallsten, *Steinbeck: A Life in Letters,* 610–11.

9. Vonnegut, *Man without a Country,* 70–71.

10. Steinbeck and Ricketts, *Sea of Cortez,* 88.

11. Lewis, *Moneyball,* 93.

12. Quoted in Meine, *Aldo Leopold,* 498.

13. Aldo Leopold, "Natural History: The Forgotten Science," in *Round River* (Minocqua, Wisc.: NorthWord Press, 1991), 92–101; this essay was previously published in *Sand County Almanac.* Thanks to Eric Engles for the referral.

14. Personal communication, March 17, 2009.

CHAPTER SEVENTEEN

1. Paul Hawken, *Blessed Unrest: How the Largest Social Movement in History is Restoring Grace, Justice, and Beauty to the World* (New York: Penguin Books, 2007).

2. Hawken, *Blessed Unrest,* 165.

3. Meine, *Aldo Leopold,* 163.

INDEX